D1008968

To

_____

_____

_____

_____

From

_____

Date

_____

A Woman After God's Own Heart

A Daily Devotional

Elizabeth George

HARVEST HOUSE PUBLISHERS

EUGENE, OREGON

Cover photo © Muneyuki Nishimura / Solus Photography / Veer

Cover by Garborg Design Works, Savage, Minnesota

A WOMAN AFTER GOD'S OWN HEART®—A DAILY DEVOTIONAL
Copyright © 2007 by Elizabeth George, published by Harvest House Publishers, Eugene, Oregon 97402, www.harvesthousepublishers.com

Library of Congress Cataloging-in-Publication Data
   George, Elizabeth, 1944-
   A woman after God's own heart : a daily devotional / Elizabeth George.
   ISBN-13: 978-0-7369-2081-0 (hardcover)
   ISBN-10: 0-7369-2081-1
   1. Devotional literature. 2. Christian women—Religious life. I. Title.
   BV4844.G432 2007
   242.' 643—dc22
                                   2007017461

Printed in China

07 08 09 10 11 12 13 14 / RDS-SK / 14 13 12 11 10 9 8 7 6 5 4 3 2 1

A Note from Elizabeth

Imagine living in such a way that people think of you as a woman after God's heart. Better yet, imagine placing God foremost in your heart each morning and striking out on His path for your day, deliberately living for Him. As you commit yourself to God each day, He will work in your heart!

I pray these 366 devotions for busy women like you will help inspire you to draw nearer to God and live out His plans for you. How is this done? The answer: via small steps with big results—living God's way...one day at a time, practicing God's order of priorities for you...one day at a time, committing the many different areas of your life to God...one day at a time.

Treat yourself to jewels of wisdom based on God's Word each day. Enjoy the scriptures and messages in this devotional created just for you, a woman who loves the Lord with all her heart. Be inspired to grow. Be willing to change. Be encouraged to take bold steps in handling your problems or facing difficulties. Most of all, become more knowledgeable of God's character and His great love for you.

May your journey to greater faith and trust in God be filled with joy and delight!

1

Golden Day Perspective

❦

"My life right now is like my 401(k)—about half its worth!" There's no question: Life can seem hopeless and pointless at times. But imagine being a woman who can treat each day as if it—and it alone—were a God-given, golden day. Looking at your day from a "golden day" perspective helps you practice priorities. And it's also "the why" that will motivate you to carry them out. Okay, what if your day has been one of failure? A day for merely surviving? Thanks be to God who enables you to forget today and reach forward to tomorrow! It's just as Philippians 3:13 NASB says, "Press on toward the goal"—again, and again, and again. Keep following after God's heart no matter what.

Lord, help me look to You when my day is going well...and when my day is looking bleak. I want to serve You and honor You in everything I do. Amen.

2

I Give Myself to You

❀

We all make choices in what we do with our day. A favorite verse of mine ends with the words, "Charm is deceitful and beauty is vain, but a woman who fears the LORD, she shall be praised" (Proverbs 31:30 NASB). I don't want to be robbed of even one of God's riches by not taking time to let Him invade my life. The bottom line? I want to be a woman after God's own heart!

Make a daily commitment to God. It can be as simple as praying, "Lord, today I give myself anew to You!" Your heart for God should be like a boiling pot—intense and passionate. There's no way to ignore that kind of fire! Be excited to meet God.

Lord, I commit my life to You. Help me be a witness to Your gracious power and love. Amen.

Stop Complaining

✤

I want to say this as nicely as possible: It's time to stop complaining. In Philippians 4:11-13 the apostle Paul writes, "I have learned to be content whatever the circumstances. I know what it is to be in need, and I know what it is to have plenty. I have learned the secret of being content in any and every situation, whether well fed or hungry, whether living in plenty or in want. I can do everything through him who gives me strength" (NIV).

Never once do we see Paul quitting, having a fit, or complaining. Regardless of his predicament, he was content. Why? Because he looked to his Savior for strength. The Bible says to be steadfast, always abounding in the work of the Lord. And when you do, you're on the way to becoming the best possible woman you can be—a woman who serves the Lord.

Lord, help me look to You for my purpose and my strength. Lead me every day so I can do Your will and serve You to the best of my ability. Amen.

Far from Perfect

"If one more thing goes wrong today…I'm outta here!" I've been there, done that. I'm sure you've been there too. In real life it's impossible to be perfect, be steadfast, and do the right thing in all circumstances. But remember King David? He was given the title "a man after God's own heart" (1 Samuel 13:14; Acts 13:22). And he was far from perfect. Does the name Bathsheba ring a bell? (See 2 Samuel 11.) Despite his forgetting to consult God, his adultery with Bathsheba, his cold-blooded arrangements to murder Uriah so he could marry Bathsheba, or his less than wonderful parenting, David was called a man after God's heart.

Don't you find this so encouraging as you continue on the path of being a woman after God's heart? This journey is an exciting one—and you'll find a lot of joy along the way.

Lord, I'm so excited about what You have in store for me. Even when I forget to turn to You, You still love me and have my best interests in mind. Thank You! Amen.

Less and Less Time

Another birthday has come...and gone. I'm painfully aware that there's less and less time for becoming the kind of woman I want to be. But it's also comforting to know that God knows the desires of my heart. In fact, Psalm 37:4 says He's put them there. He knows the daydreaming—and praying—I do about serving Him. And He knows your heart too. Whether you're pushing a stroller, a grocery cart, or an aluminum walker—your life counts. It counts mightily as you face life's challenges with a heart full of devotion to God. Keep choosing to love God, and follow after Him with a whole heart each day.

Lord, in You is my hope, in You is my desire, in You is my strength. I love You. Make my life count in someone's life today. Help me reach out with Your love. Amen.

6

The One Thing Needed

❦

Remember the story of Martha and Mary when Jesus came to dinner? Imagine God coming to your house! Who wouldn't be rattled? But Martha was so busy she crossed the line of graciously providing food and became overly involved in hosting. When Mary slipped out of the kitchen to sit quietly at Jesus' feet, Martha broke under the anger she was feeling. She was so busy doing things for the Lord, she failed to spend time with Him. She went to the Lord and complained. And what was His reply? "Martha, Martha, you are worried and bothered about so many things; but only one thing is necessary, for Mary has chosen the good part, which shall not be taken away from her" (Luke 10:41-42).

Does this sound familiar? Choose the "one thing" necessary. Be in Christ's presence constantly, seeking after Him.

Lord, at times it seems impossible for me to stay focused on You. But I know with Your great love You reach down to me so I can reach up to You. I praise Your name! Amen.

He Will Direct Your Path

Proverbs 3:6 says, "In all your ways acknowledge Him, and He shall direct your paths." But what does that look like in your daily life? The phone rings and it's bad news or a decision needs to be made. This is where you stop and pray, "God, what do You want me to do here?" Or you're going merrily through your day—and someone says something that really hurts. Before you blurt out a smart retort, sit mentally in God's presence. Ask, "Okay, God, what do You want me to say?" When you do your part, God takes over and does His part: He directs your path…and your mouth! Isn't that great?

Heavenly Father, thank You for meeting me where I am. You care about the big things in my life and You care about the little things. You are amazing! Amen.

8

Accepting Christ

❧

I pray you've given your heart to the Lord. That you've entered into an eternal relationship with God through His Son, Jesus Christ. My dear sister, if you're unsure about where you stand with God, invite Jesus to be your Savior. When you do, you're welcoming Christ into your life. You become a "new creature" (2 Corinthians 5:17 NASB). All it takes is acknowledging your sin before God. Your prayer might be: "God I want to be Your child, a true woman after Your heart. I acknowledge my sin and receive Your Son, Jesus Christ, into my needy heart, giving thanks that He died on the cross for my sins."

Lord, thank You for hearing my prayer. Thank You for coming to earth so I can be in communion with You. I love You. Amen.

Under the Surface

❈

Alaskan fishermen will tell you that only one-seventh of an iceberg is visible above the surface. Remember the *Titanic?* It crashed into an iceberg because the majority of it was hidden underneath. An iceberg is an awesome force in nature and should be held in great respect. And in a way, that's exactly what you and I should want for our lives. The public part of our lives as women of God should stir up awe and wonder. And our strength should be explained by what goes on in private between us and God.

I don't know about you, but I want people to marvel at what they see of God in me—to be in awe of a woman who serves God wholeheartedly.

Lord, help me draw closer to You every day. I want to be Your light that shines so brightly that people will be drawn to Your love and power. Amen.

People Noise

✤

Sometimes I get tired of listening. But the truth is that we're surrounded by people. At work, on campus, at church, at home. I heard one wise person say, "You can't be with people all of the time and have a ministry to people." Frankly, that's encouraging. If part of your day is spent hidden in reflection, in prayer, in preparation, your effectiveness will be even greater. It's interesting, isn't it? The impact of your ministry to people will be in direct proportion to the time you spend away from people and with God. Be a woman who makes wise decisions regarding her time.

Lord, remind me to spend quality and quantity time with You this week. Help me stay focused so I can serve You in everything I do. Amen.

Roots Run Deep

When my mother-in-law was seriously ill, my husband—her only son—was out of the country and unreachable. As I cared for her by the hour, I have to tell you—I was reaching deep into my reservoir! There just wasn't time for my usual quiet times with God. What I found was strength in the many scriptures I'd memorized over the years. I gained energy from the psalms I'd read and from past times I spent alone with God. Those were roots deep into God's truth. And I needed every one of them.

If you're going to be a woman after God's own heart, the support you get from a healthy root system is vital for standing strong in the Lord. Meet with God regularly. Talk to Him through prayer and commune with Him through meditation. Read His wisdom found in His Word.

Heavenly Father, thank You for loving me and caring about me daily. I love that I can come to You in times of stress and weakness, and You will give me strength. Amen.

12

Something Is Better Than Nothing

If someone asked you to describe your quiet time with God today, what would you say? We know how to pull off parties, weddings, and retreats. And our quiet times should be no different—especially considering the value. What's ideal for you? What would make them quality times? What energizes and refreshes you? Keep in mind that something is always better than nothing. Pick a time that matches your lifestyle—even if it's the middle of the night…or at a lunch break… or in the car. Take out your calendar and make an appointment each day.

Meeting with God is such a vital part of becoming all He created you to be!

Father, it's so hard sometimes to set aside time to meet with You. Life is so demanding—family, friends, work, meetings all pull at me. Time seems so short. Please help me keep my priorities in order so I meet with You every day. Thank You. Amen.

13

Dream Big

❋

Hmm…1 year…12 months…365 days. That's 8,760 hours! You've got time. So dream big. Dream of being a woman who serves and honors God. Will you do this?

First, describe the woman you want to be—spiritually, that is—in one year. In one year you can attack a weak area in your Christian life and gain victory. You can read through the Bible. You can be mentored by an older woman…or be a mentor to a younger woman in the faith. You can complete training in evangelism or finish a one-year Bible study. You can memorize Scripture. Dawson Trotman was a great Christian statesman. He memorized one verse a day for the first three years of his Christian life—that's a thousand verses! Dream on—and do it!

Lord, I hesitate to dream because I'm afraid of commitment and failure. What if I start out and then get tired or forget? But, Lord, I want to grow in You. I want to become the person You want me to be. Give me a dream…and the strength and passion to carry it out. Amen.

14

The Perfect Diet

I cut out the obituary of a young composer who made himself work on his music at least 600 hours each year. He tracked it in a diary so he could see each day's progress. Imagine what kind of transformation would occur in your heart if you spent this amount of time—or even more—each day drawing near to God through His Word. What life-changing value it would have for eternity! Will you do that today? Purpose in your heart to spend more time reading the Bible? What a joy it'll be when you grow to love God's Word more than food for your body. It's the perfect diet!

Lord, my love affair with food will be hard to break. Although everyone needs food, help me see that Your Word is what is truly life giving. Today I purpose to spend some time each day in Your Word. Amen.

15

The Woman of Your Dreams

❧

God will take you as far as you want to go—as fast as you want to go. To be that woman of your dreams, that woman after God's own heart, is up to you. Proverbs 4:23 says, "Keep your heart with all diligence, for out of it spring the issues of life." You decide what you will or will not do—whether you'll grow or not. And you also decide the rate at which you'll grow. Will it be hit and miss? Or what I call the measles rate: a sudden rash here and there? Do you believe you can be a woman of God? With God's grace and in His strength you can.

Lord, I want to be Your woman…a woman who loves and serves You. Give me the wisdom and perseverance to grow in my relationship with You. Thank You for giving me this opportunity. Amen.

A Prayer Makeover

❖

I remember the day as if it were yesterday. It was my tenth spiritual birthday. I'd dropped my children off at school and was at my desk—resting before God and rejoicing for being His child. I thought back over the years and, with tears of gratitude, prayed, "Lord, what do You see missing in my spiritual life?" The immediate response was all too clear: "Your prayer life!" That day I wrote in my journal, "I dedicate and purpose to spend the next ten years developing a meaningful prayer life." What a rewarding time it has been putting into motion a complete prayer makeover. And in the process becoming a woman who heartily loves and serves God.

Father, thank You for hearing my prayers. It's so exciting to reach up to You on my own…to not have to go through anybody or anything to talk and listen to You. Amen.

Gossip

For me, gossip was a serious struggle. Oh I knew God spoke specifically to women who gossip. I did it anyway. I tried everything to break myself of this habit. I taped little notes on the telephone like: Is it true? Is it kind? Is it helpful? I prayed about gossiping each day, and still I did it. I was so sick of failing. I finally reached the point where I asked God to do radical surgery. Real change only began when I started to confess gossip as a sin—each time I did it. I've had some lapses since then, but confession of sin was a turning point. With God's help, gossip no longer has such a hold on me. Praise the Lord!

Lord Jesus, it's so easy to get caught up in hearing negatives about other people and sharing them with others...sometimes in the guise of "please pray for so and so." Help me focus on building others up...not tearing anyone down. Amen.

18

What a Difference

Maybe you can relate. My phone would ring at nine o'clock. When I answered it, a woman would make a perfectly reasonable request. I'd be full of energy and blurt out, "Sure! When do you want me?" At four o'clock that afternoon, the phone would ring again with someone else asking the same basic thing and I'd say...or at least think, "No way!" Why did I respond so differently? In a word—"feelings"! My decisions were based on how I felt at the moment. I wasn't making spiritual decisions; I was making physical decisions. And that's not the way to follow God. Out of desperation I developed a motto for myself: "Make no decision without prayer." Try it! Imagine the difference it will make in your life.

Lord, please remind me to pray before I make any decisions. My life is Yours, and I want to do and serve how and where You want me to. Amen.

You Didn't Need It

❖

When my husband, Jim, was in seminary, we lived in a tiny house with peeling paint and a living room ceiling about to cave in. All our income went for tuition, rent, and groceries. I desperately needed victory in the area of my heart's desires and dreams. Over and over again I placed everything in God's hands. And a prayer principle was born: "If God doesn't meet it, you didn't need it."

Through the years God has faithfully met the many needs of our family. We've experienced the reality of God's promise that "no good thing will He withhold from those who walk uprightly" (Psalm 84:11). And it's true for you too!

Lord, thank You for watching over me and providing for me and those I love. I appreciate all You've done for me, all that You are doing for me, and all that You will do for me. I love You! Amen.

A Heart that Obeys

❧

I'll never forget the time my daughter wanted to impress her boyfriend—and us—by making brownies. Expecting something wonderful, we had to keep from making faces as we bit into the much-awaited brownies. They were horrible! What happened? When we asked whether she'd done anything special or unique in the baking process, my daughter volunteered, "Oh, I left out the salt. Salt's not good for you."

Because of one missing ingredient the whole batch had to be tossed out. Just as that batch of brownies required several ingredients to become what it was intended to be—there's an ingredient key to us becoming women who follow God's heart. The heart God delights in is one that is compliant, cooperative, and responsive to Him—a heart that obeys!

Lord, so many times I want to do what I want to do…so I don't consult You or think about what I know to be true according to Your Word. Please help me remember that serving and loving You are my top priorities. Amen.

When You're Unsure

❖

What about those situations where you're just not sure what's right? In your heart, you want to do the correct thing, but what is that? First of all, don't do anything until you know what's right. Ask God for guidance. Take time to pray, to think, to search the Scriptures. And ask advice from someone more seasoned in Christ. Remember, if a person is asking you to do something you're unsure of, you can simply say, "I'm going to have to give this some thought and pray about it. I'll let you know later." Then do so!

Lord, I'm so glad I can come to You for wisdom and guidance. It makes life so much easier and a lot more interesting when I'm following You and doing what You want me to do. Amen.

Stop Doing Wrong

❧

Are you doing something that is wrong? Today I'm urging you to stop. I can't make it any simpler than that. The split second you think or do anything that will displease God's heart, stop immediately! This action will train your heart to be responsive to God in all situations. If you gossip—stop. If you think unworthy thoughts—stop. If you have a spark of anger—stop before you act on it. Everyone has experiences like these. They happen to all of us often. But how you respond reveals what's at the core of your heart. Call on the Lord. First John 1:9 promises God is "faithful and just to forgive us our sins and to cleanse us from all unrighteousness."

Father God, You are amazing! Not only are You faithful and just to forgive me my sins, but You also cover me with Your grace when I fail to live up to Your standards. Thank You for Your mercy. Amen.

Confessing Sin

"Hi! Are you one of the new guys?"

"No, but I'm one of the new girls!"

Those were my exact words said with all the sarcasm I could muster. And I was responding to a woman who was trying to be friendly and welcome me to the church choir! We've all spoken inappropriately. We've said something in anger or without thought. When you do, admit your wrongful behavior to the person you've hurt. And when you confess your sin, be sure you're also forsaking it. Don't be like the farmer who said, "I want to confess I stole some hay from my neighbor." When he was asked, "How much did you steal?" the farmer replied, "I stole half a load, but make it a whole load. I'm going back to get the other half tonight!"

Jesus, when I've thoughtlessly or even deliberately hurt someone's feelings, please point it out to me immediately. Give me the courage to ask You for forgiveness and then go to the person I've wronged to seek his or her forgiveness. Amen.

A Servant Woman

First Peter 4:10 says, "Each one should use whatever gift he has received to serve others, faithfully administering God's grace in its various forms." If you're not married, this means you serve God, your family and friends, the company you work for, and people at church and in the community. If you're married, this servant attitude starts with your husband.

It took a few years, but I finally figured out that I'm on assignment from God to help my husband, Jim. I can honestly say I became a better wife—and a better Christian—when I became a better helper. According to God's plan, I'm not to compete, but to be solidly behind my husband. I'm to be supportive. How does this translate into daily life? Jim is the one I'm supposed to help first, to assist in making his every victory possible.

Lord, I'm so selfish most of the time. Help me combat this tendency and look to You for the strength and wisdom to set my own wants and desires aside and serve the people You've asked me to serve. Amen.

A Sign of Maturity

❉

Do you have a servant attitude? It's hard at times, isn't it? But we're called to serve one another. The apostle Paul reminds us of this in Galatians 5: "For you were called to freedom, brethren; only do not turn your freedom into an opportunity for the flesh, but through love serve one another" (verses 13-14). Having a servant attitude—especially toward your husband if you're married—is a sure sign of maturity. How do you measure up as a helper? Are you a team player? What about those competitive thoughts or desires?

Our service to others glorifies God. It reflects the love He's given to us and to the world, encouraging people in our spheres of influence to seek Him too. This simple and noble assignment to be loving servants comes from God and reaps rich rewards!

Father, help me keep my ego in check and focus on the needs of others. I want people to feel my love and know it comes from You. I want to be a light that draws people to You. Amen.

26

A Single Head

❀

"If it wouldn't kill you—I'd like my lunch now!" Do you know any husbands who have this attitude? When the Bible talks about a husband being the head of the house, this is not what God's Word had in mind! "Head of the house" simply means your husband is the one who is ultimately responsible before God for his leadership decisions. As a wife, you are accountable for how you follow that leadership. When I was a child I visited a museum that had the stuffed head of a goat—only it had two heads. It was freakish, abnormal, and ugly. And so is a marriage with two heads. God, the perfect artist, designed marriage to be beautiful, natural, and functional. He did it by giving it a single head—the husband.

God, You designed marriage. It's so hard sometimes to let my husband be the head of our home. Please give him wisdom and a gentle spirit. And help me respond to him as I would respond to You. Amen.

Submission?

❧

"It's time I did something for me for a change!"
Sue wanted to quit her job for full-time ministry, and
she came to me for counsel. When I asked what her
husband had to say, she said, "Oh, he's not a Christian.
He doesn't want me to do it." Others told Sue to go
ahead and pursue her dream, but the Bible is clear in
its instructions. Wives are to "submit" to their own
husbands (Ephesians 5:22).

As long as your husband isn't asking you to violate
God's Word, as a woman who serves Him, you are to
submit. It's by faith in a sovereign God that you and
I trust Him to work in our lives directly through our
husbands. It may not be popular today, but it's a truth
found in the Bible.

*Jesus, create in my heart the desire to serve my
husband…and the other people You've placed in my
life. Give me the strength, patience, and gentleness I
need to fully model Your love to them. Amen.*

Make Your Husband #1

❧

Talk to your mother about recipes, skills, interests, the Bible, and spiritual growth—but not about your husband. If you haven't already, decide right now to make your husband your Number One human relationship. And that includes making him a priority over your children. Counselors will tell you that the point where marriages most often jump the track is in overinvesting in children and underinvesting in the marriage. Ask yourself, "Am I spoiling my husband rotten?" There's nothing wrong with doing everything in your power to please your husband. That's what loving him is all about. Invest your time, your heart, and your life in prayer for your husband. It's impossible to hate or neglect a person you're praying for!

Lord, help me look at my husband with fresh, loving eyes. I want to see anew all his good qualities...all the things that drew me to him. Give me opportunities to remind him that I love him and why. Amen.

Plan Romance

✤

"Dinner for two? I don't think he's been home in time for dinner in the last month!" Nothing just happens...including a great marriage. Proverbs 21:5 says, "Good planning and hard work lead to prosperity" (NLT). And never is that more true than in a marriage. Plan what I like to call "special deeds of kindness." Run an errand for your husband. Cheer him up. Plan special dinners—dinners he likes. And create special times alone so you can talk and enjoy one another's company. If you're starting to avoid those cozy times—make plans right now to remedy the situation. Loving your husband is part of becoming a woman after God's own heart. Go ahead—lavish love on that husband of yours!

Lord, spark my creativity and help me show my husband how much I love him. Guide me as I make him a priority and encourage him to put time with me on his schedule. Amen.

Coming Home to Me!

✺

If company were coming you'd do a little something to freshen up, wouldn't you? Well, your husband is more precious and special than company! Run a comb through your hair, freshen your makeup, and change your clothes so he's not seeing the same old jogging outfit you had on when he left in the morning. Put on a bright color and some lipstick. A spritz of perfume wouldn't hurt either. The most important person in your life is about to walk through the door. Prepare the children too so he receives a warm, loving welcome. Martin Luther once said, "Let the wife make her husband glad to come home!" What great advice!

Lord, some days are so harried that it's hard to take the time to look good for my man. I'm going to pay more attention to how I look when I greet him. I want him to know how much I love the fact that he comes home to me. Amen.

Being a Wise Mom

Before I was a Christian I focused my time and energy on pursuing a counseling license to help other families. Unfortunately, I was neglecting my own. I was happy being my own woman and pursuing my own dreams. But one night I was invited to a women's Bible study. I heard comments about "the joy of loving my children," "the privilege of motherhood," and the "awesome responsibility" of raising children for God. I discovered that one of my God-given roles was to train and discipline my kids. God opened my eyes to what it means to be a wise and loving mom. There's no greater ministry than that of being a mother.

Lord, I want my children to love me and think only good thoughts about me, so it's hard to discipline them. But training and obedience are so important to character development. Give me wisdom and guidance as I love my children. Amen.

32

A Heart Response

🌺

Your husband is your life mate. God's given you that husband of yours for your personal fulfillment, for companionship, and, more importantly, for your spiritual development. It's true! Your Christian character becomes evident every time you choose from your heart to bend, to yield, to honor him and his decisions. And I'm not talking about giving an "Oh, okay," response. I'm talking about offering a positive, encouraging heart response, an enthusiastic "Sure!" Submission to your husband is one way you honor God. Look into God's face and then submit to your husband as to the Lord. It will bring a beauty to your life that reflects your heart!

Lord, search my heart and show me any area where I refuse to submit to You or my husband. Help me understand Your will and give me the strength to follow through. Thank You for my husband. I love him…and I love You. Amen.

Developing a Passion for God

❦

I'm sure you have a deep and abiding passion for God's Word. And if you're a mom, you want your kids to know and love God. The Bible says, "Faith comes by hearing and hearing by the Word of God" (Romans 10:17). God's Word provides the knowledge and wisdom your children need to accept Jesus. And if you develop in them a habit of reading the Bible, it will guide them their whole lives! So, as a mother, place God's Holy Scripture first on the list of things your children need to know. And first in your own heart as well. Your passion for Scripture will spill over as you teach your children about Jesus.

Lord, thank You for the incredible blessing of children. I give my precious ones to You. Open their hearts to You and to Your Word. Help me present Your love and guidance in a way that will make them yearn to know You. Amen.

Laugh and Smile a Lot

❀

Your home should be an absolute joy for every family member! I've learned to smile—and laugh—a lot. When my girls were little, we'd check out silly riddle books from the library and then laugh and roll on the floor as we read them. Try it!

I also use the words "I love" freely: "I love Saturdays." "I love the Lord's Day." "I love everything—and especially I love you!" I say those very words to my husband, Jim, my two daughters and their husbands, and now my seven grandkids every time I see them, tell them goodbye, or talk to them on the phone. Ask God to fill your heart with love and give you plenty of opportunities to laugh and play!

Lord, I imagine Your smile and joy as the children came up and You took them into Your arms and blessed them. What love and acceptance You showed them! Help me do the same for my kids…and for any other children You bring into my life. Amen.

Family First

"Hurry up, girls. We're late as it is!"

I was on a mission of mercy and hurrying my two girls to the car. We were delivering a meal for a friend who'd just had a baby. I'd spent most of the morning preparing a special basket of delicious food. As we started out the door, one of my daughters wanted to know what we were doing and why. I was feeling quite happy with myself as I shared our goal until Katherine asked, "What are we having for dinner?"

As I thought about my plan to throw together something quick and easy for my own family I realized that my priorities weren't exactly in the right order. I was making a special effort to create a delicious meal for someone else…and my own family was getting the short shrift. Ouch!

Lord, You come first in my life…and then comes my family. Help me live those priorities in everything I do—including fixing meals. Amen.

Teach Your Children

❧

What are you teaching your children by the things you say? By what you do? By the places you go? As a mother who knows God, you have the privilege of raising your children to love and follow God. And for that to happen, you have to talk about God to your children—and then back your teachings up with your actions. After all, we talk and do what's important to us. And when we talk about and follow God's rules we communicate that He's supremely important to us. Even though children have "selective hearing" at times, the message gets through! So how's your talk? How's your walk?

Lord, it's easy to get caught up in daily duties and forget my children are watching how I think, act, and handle emotions. Help me model Your love, Your values, and Your principles so they'll grow to be loving and responsible. Amen.

Love Covers All Sins

❀

"Teenagers! Ugh!" Have you heard someone say something like this? I have. But the Proverbs 31 mother "opens her mouth with wisdom, and on her tongue is the law of kindness" (verse 26). We communicate volumes about our homes and our hearts every time we broadcast harmful criticism or attitudes about our children. My friend Betty taught me a lesson I'll never forget. She'd say, "Elizabeth, how old are the girls now?" When I answered, "Nine and ten," she'd exclaim, "Oh I remember when my boys were nine and ten. What wonderful years!" What an encouragement to me! Betty was a mother whose heart was filled with motherly affection. Her heart was positive about God's job assignment for her and her lips were respectfully quiet about any difficulties. Proverbs 10:12 says, "Love covers all sins!"

Lord, when the kids are running wild, the house is a mess, and I feel stretched to the limit, please calm my spirit. Give me Your grace and patience. Remind me what a joy and privilege it is to be a mom. Amen.

The Power of Prayer

✦

"Mom, thanks for praying for me today. It really made a difference!" How blessed we are as mothers to pray for our dear children. And what a delight to set the tone in your home—one of love and laughter, fun and prayer. God makes your heart joyful, generous, giving, happy, and quiet. He enables you to focus on and live out your priorities. And He provides what you need to go the extra mile as a wife and mom. It's not an easy job assignment, but Philippians 4:13 promises that you can do all things through Christ who strengthens you. So lift your heart and your voice to God today. Praise Him for His faithfulness. Thank Him for loving you and for loving your family.

Lord, You are so wonderful. You give me what I need…and then You fulfill the desires of my heart. Thank You for my husband and for my children. You are amazing! Amen.

A Wake-Up Call

❋

There's nothing like the reality of an alarm clock! It's definitely a wake-up call. It reminds me that as a woman I'm responsible for the quality of life in the home my family lives in. What I've discovered is that I'm the thermostat. I regulate the "temperature" in our home—making it quiet, joyful, loving, and supportive. These things don't just happen because I hope they will. The best way to provide a cheerful, loving, positive, and constructive home is to go to God's Word each morning and pray—giving God the opportunity to set the temperature of my heart to match His. It will work for you too!

Lord, what an awesome responsibility You've placed in my hands. It's critical that I meet with You every day to get my husband, my children, and me started right. Thank You for being available and willing to be part of our lives! Amen.

A Place of Refuge

❊

"If I can just get home everything will be okay!" Wouldn't it be great if every member of your family knew there was one place where "everything will be all right"? Your home should be a place of refuge. A place for healing. A place for renewal. Look around your house or apartment…inside and out. Make a list of the things that need to be added, repaired, or set up to create an ambiance of a peaceful haven.

And don't forget your attitude. That's where we're sometimes put to the test. What is that one attitude that if it were improved—transformed by God— would enhance the feel of your home?

I encourage you to take a new look at your home and how people interact there. Take whatever steps you need to improve the sometimes calm, sometimes fun, and always supportive atmosphere at home.

Jesus, I so appreciate having a place my family and I can call home. Bless everyone who walks in our doors. I want my home to echo Your love and care. Amen.

Say Nothing

"Ron? Who cares what he says?" We've all met women who don't respect their husbands. They nag, pick apart, and disagree with their mates…and don't care who hears. I've seen a woman like this correct every little thing her husband did. "No, George, it wasn't eight years ago—it was seven!" Or she cut him off, interrupted, or—even worse—finished his sentences.

If we're serving God, we need to be respectful, loving, and considerate. Many times all we have to do to give a positive response is to say nothing. It took me a while, but I finally realized my mouth doesn't always have to be moving. I don't always have to express my opinions. Is this hitting a little close to home?

Jesus, Proverbs 21:23 says, "Whoever guards his mouth and tongue keeps his soul from troubles." Help me remember this truth! Show me when I'm being disrespectful so that I can shift course. I want to honor You and uplift others with my speech. Amen.

Watch and Act

Eighteenth-century preacher Jonathan Edwards was blessed to have a wife who watched over his home. Sarah was most definitely a woman who followed God in her thoughts and deeds. And she proved it in the way she supported her husband. One day Jonathan looked up from his studies and asked Sarah, "Isn't it about time for the hay to be cut?" Because she stood guard over what was precious in her life, she was able to say, "It's been in the barn for two weeks!"

What a blessing you can be as you watch, as you keep a lookout for what's needed in your home. And what a great way to be a helper for your husband—to anticipate, perceive, and act on his needs and wants.

God, open my eyes to what's going on around me. Show me creative ways that I can be more organized and helpful. Thank You for caring about even the little, everyday aspects of my life. Amen.

Time Robbers

Do you want to use your time effectively and honor God? Then guard your time carefully. What "time robbers" are in your life? The first one is a ringing phone. You don't always have to answer it! Let the answering machine pick it up. Another problem is being interrupted. Tell people you'll get back to them…and set up a time that's convenient. Failing to delegate also wastes time. And unclear priorities mean you'll probably go on fruitless tangents.

Which of these robbers will you tackle this week so you'll be more efficient and effective as a believer, a woman, a wife, a mother, and a professional?

Oh, and one more thing: Your children are not interruptions. They are your greatest work and the best investment of your time.

Father, I complain I don't have enough hours in my day. I don't get my chores done, I get behind at work, I skip my Bible study, I throw something together for dinner. With Your help I want to be more focused, more efficient, more consistent. Amen.

From House to Home

❧

"Oh for the good old days when I had no kids!" I think all parents have thought this at one time or another. I encourage you to take a close look at the terrific work you do for your family. Do you count the value of every meal prepared? Every rug vacuumed? Every floor mopped? Sadly, far too few houses have been made into homes. Check your heart attitude toward your place. My friend Ginger goes through her entire house, praying that each room will be filled with God's love and protection. This definitely puts a new slant on housework!

Praise God for your home and the people who live with you. Ask Him to fill your heart with His desires for your home. And don't forget to request a renewed sense of purpose and the strength needed to persevere.

Father, it's hard to keep a positive attitude about mundane chores. Often my work isn't even acknowledged. Remind me that my joy is in You, and that everything I do has a purpose and glorifies You in some way. Amen.

Diet and Exercise

Every time I ask a woman who's enjoying an energetic life and ministry how she does it, I cringe. Two words are always the predictable answer: diet and exercise. Were you hoping this subject wouldn't come up? We're told in the Bible that how we manage our body affects our ministries and the quality of our lives. The apostle Paul put it this way: "I discipline my body and bring it into subjection, lest, when I have preached to others, I myself should become disqualified" (1 Corinthians 9:27). If your goal is a quality of life filled with quality days of serving the Lord, attention to your body is key!

Father, the human body is so complex and intricate. What amazing creatures You created! Because I want to be a good steward of the body You gave me, I'm going to start exercising in some way and eating more nutritious foods. Please watch over me and guard my health. Amen.

There You Are!

I love what author Anne Ortlund says: "There are two kinds of personalities—and you are one of the two. People can tell which, as soon as you walk into a room: your attitude says either 'Here I am' or 'There you are.'" A great illustration of this is a Hawaiian woman who strings a number of flower leis early each Sunday morning. She comes to church praying, "Lord, who needs my leis today? A newcomer? Someone discouraged? Lead me to the right people."

Are you a "there you are" person? Are you looking around for how you can encourage someone with God's love? He can make it happen as you let Him guide you.

God, You've given me so much. To honor You and show my appreciation, lead me to people with whom I can share the gifts You've given me. Give me opportunities to share how they can have a personal relationship with You through Your Son Jesus. Amen.

Reading Promotes Growth

There was a time when reading was more popular than watching TV. Imagine that! Are you wondering, Who has time to read? Ruth Graham told her daughters, "Keep reading and you'll be educated!" It's easy to think you don't have time to read, but simply carrying a book everywhere you go gets many books read. I used to set my timer and read for just five minutes a day. It may not sound like much, but I've gone through many books this way! Reading can play an important role in your spiritual growth. Of course the Bible is the primary book you should read, but the books of women such as Ruth Graham, Edith Schaeffer, Elisabeth Elliot, and Anne Ortlund are also good. When you read their books, you are being mentored!

God, as I read my Bible this week open my eyes so I can grasp Your wisdom and principles for life. Help me incorporate them into my life. And also lead me to books that will help me love You and the people around me more thoroughly. Amen.

48

God's Timing

❦

I'm tempted at times to think my quiet time with God doesn't matter. That it doesn't count. Nobody sees it, and sometimes it feels like there's no glory, no attention given to the weeks, months, and years of waiting on God. Can you relate? After all, few people, if any, see you reading God's Word. No one's there to watch you memorize and meditate on God's life-changing truths.

Let me encourage you! God sees you on bended knee in prayer. He uses your dedication and openness to prepare you for ministry. And He will present those opportunities in His time. Right now, you're responsible for cooperating with God's efforts to prepare you. So clear your calendar. Set aside some time to place yourself before God. Wait on Him!

God, today I pray Psalm 119:27 to You: "Make me understand the way of Your precepts; so shall I meditate on Your wonderful works." Open my eyes and my heart to Your wisdom, Father, and give me Your directions today. Amen.

Never Dull

❀

Picture a woman you really admire and then describe her. Most likely she's stimulating, challenging, energetic, and joyful. She motivates you, and you enjoy being with her. She's growing and willing to share what she's learning. And she's never dull!

I hope you know at least one woman like this, someone who is a fervent woman after God's own heart. This gal has spent time with God, and when she's in public she can't help but share her love of Jesus. And that's the bottom line, you know. That's where real joy comes from—time spent with the Lord.

You can be that kind of woman! Let the Lord enrich you and prepare you for ministry.

Lord, it's so exciting to spend time with You. Thank You for making the ultimate sacrifice so I can have an intimate relationship with You. Help me focus on You. I want to worship You and bless others all day long. Amen.

50

The Power of Giving

Sometimes your presence is worth a thousand words. Be a giver. A smile, a greeting, a warm question, a hug can go a long way in making someone feel accepted and appreciated. And don't just give—give liberally, cheerfully, above and beyond the normal "Hi." Proverbs 3:27 gives a word to the wise: "Do not withhold good from those to whom it is due, when it is in the power of your hand to do so." Offer words of praise, encouragement, thanks, and kindness. Send a note of appreciation. Sharing blessings with others is a choice. Choose to make a difference today!

God, You designed me for fellowship with You and with other people. As I commune with You and meet with people, I want to give my undivided attention so I communicate clearly and lovingly. Amen.

51

Be All There

❧

Wherever you are, be all there! Live life to the hilt in every situation you believe to be the will of God. Go expecting God to use you. Go to give, to reach out. Withhold nothing. Be what one woman calls a "hanger-arounder." As long as you've already set aside the time and made the effort to go to an event, give totally and freely. Minister to as many people as you can in as many ways as you can. It's a surefire way to glorify and serve God! A friend and I have made a pact: When we find ourselves gravitating toward each other at an event or a party, one of us will announce: "C'mon! Let's go touch some sheep."

Lord, I want to tell everyone what a wonderful God You are. If I'm tired, give me strength. If I'm feeling shy, give me courage. If I'm hesitant, give me the right words to say. Thank You. Amen.

52

Memorizing God's Word

❁

Want a great way to honor God? Memorize His Word! Before you say it let me just tell you: It's never been easy for me either. I was in a friend's home and their parrot sang *Jingle Bells*…in its entirety! As I stood there amazed at what I was hearing, I thought, Well if a parrot can learn *Jingle Bells*, I can memorize Scripture! Think of the time it took for someone to sit with that bird and teach it the melody and words of a song. Surely you can learn a verse or two from God's Word. If you do—your filled heart will be a source of encouragement to many!

Lord, turn on my brain and help me absorb Your Word today. And then give me the desire and gumption to put Your wisdom and precepts into practice and share it with others. Amen.

Be an Encourager

At church this week, look around. Who's absent? Who's traveling? Who's ill? Then sit down and write a note to that person. I can hear you saying already, "Elizabeth, you've got to be kidding. I don't have that kind of time." Here's a simple approach. Look that piece of notepaper right in the eye and say to yourself, "Just three sentences!" This will get you going. An "I miss you. I appreciate you. I'm thinking of you" works great. It doesn't get any easier than that. Carry a writing packet with you, and when you have a minute, send off a note. Be an encourager!

Father, with the advent of e-mail it's hard to take the time to jot a note to someone and mail it. But my computer isn't always handy, and I know getting handwritten notes is a special treat. Today I'll pick up some cards and stamps and look for people to encourage in Your name. Amen.

Firstfruits

With so much going on in our busy lives it's easy to get our priorities out of whack. Set aside some time this week to read and meditate on Psalm 63, where David cries out to God in the wilderness: "O God, You are my God; early will I seek You; my soul thirsts for You; my flesh longs for You in a dry and thirsty land where there is no water."

Today is the perfect time to get back on track with God. Use the firstfruits of your time to be filled spiritually so you can serve God and His people. Let people be refreshed by you. Put simply, seek first things first—every day!

Father God, my soul longs for You. Fill me with Your love so I'm no longer thirsty. Then let me minister to others, offering them living water—Your Son, Jesus. Amen.

Showing Mercy

❦

Is there someone who could use your encouragement today? A loved one? Someone who's away from family and friends? Mercy is a quality that's required of us if we're going to love and serve God. And it's something we're uniquely equipped to do as women. After all, our Lord Jesus modeled it for us so many years ago, and we're to follow His steps. Commit now to rekindle your efforts to show mercy and to serve others with all your heart. Matthew 5:7 reads, "Blessed are the merciful, for they shall obtain mercy."

Lord, give me a heart of compassion. Help me notice the needs of people around me and discover how I can ease their burdens, even if it's only in small ways. I want to reflect Your love and care to them. Amen.

God Uses Teachers

❊

Make no mistake—you are a teacher. For instance, gossip may seem like a little thing because many people do it. When you choose not to gossip you stand out and teach other women the beauty of obedience to God's wisdom: "A gossip goes around revealing secrets, but those who are trustworthy can keep a confidence" (Proverbs 11:13 NLT). When you say, "I want to ask my husband about that," you show other wives how to make their husbands a priority. When you plan your day around your children's schedules, you model for other moms respect and consideration for their children. You don't have to be a leader to teach. People will be watching you, and hopefully they'll be encouraged in their own quest to follow God. You have a powerful teaching ministry!

Lord, please give me patience and gentleness as I model Your love and values to those around me. I want to be an encourager, someone who uplifts others. With a grateful heart I want to share the joy of Your presence. Amen.

Choices

✤

The importance of choices cannot be overestimated. If you want to know what you'll be like in the future, check out the choices you're making today. What you're doing now, so you will be then. It's something of a riddle. Over time your choices change…for the better, I hope! The choices you make right now will determine whether or not you fulfill God's design for your life. Whatever you're dealing with right this minute, the next five minutes, the next hour, tomorrow, or forever—make positive decisions to love, honor, and serve the Lord. Make the choices that will alter your world…and the lives of others in positive ways.

Lord, every time I turn around I have to make decisions. Should I get up? Should I eat this or that? Should I discipline my kids? Should I buy this? Should I volunteer for this project? Please give me guidance so I will choose Your path and do Your will. Amen.

Wisdom Waits

❉

Proverbs 19:2 warns, "A person who moves too quickly may go the wrong way" (NLT). In today's fast-paced world, circumstances may try to keep you from taking the time you need to think through situations. Your kids shout that they're going to a friend's house as they head out the door. Your girlfriend calls and says she's got tickets to a concert…and do you want to go…but you have to decide right this minute 'cause they're going fast. A salesperson comes to the door and says if you order right now, you'll get a big discount on carpet cleaning.

No matter what the pressure is, "wisdom waits"! Take time to pray and, when necessary, consult someone you trust. The truth is that very few things in life call for an instant decision or offer rewards worth the problems that haste often brings. Keep your cool. Take your time.

Lord, give me a few minutes to catch my breath. Help me slow down so I can seek Your wisdom and consider the options for the decisions I have to make. Amen.

One Day at a Time

"Be calm. All you have to do is take one day at a time." I remind myself of this quite often as I look at my planner. How about you? Do you just let things happen? Many people do. And then they wonder why God doesn't seem to use them in effective ministry. To get control in your life is going to take some careful planning. Take life one day at a time. Use a day planner or something similar. Map out the next day's appointments, meetings, menus, and carpool assignments.

Tonight, when you slip under the covers, ask God to bless the next day and guide you through it. Then turn off the light. In the morning welcome the day with the psalmist's words of praise: "This is the day the LORD has made; [I] will rejoice and be glad in it!"

Lord, You've given me today. I want to enjoy doing Your will every minute. Psalm 119 says Your Word is a lamp unto my feet. Thank You for showing me Your ways. Amen.

60

Your Prayer List

Today why don't you create a brand-new prayer list? On one side of a folded piece of paper write the word "God." Then pray, "Lord, what can I do today to live out the fact that You are the ultimate priority in my life?" Then, if married, write your husband's name down. Pray, "God, what can I do today to let my husband know he is my most important human priority?" Keep adding to your list. You'll quickly discover a new enthusiasm for God and a new zeal for prayer. And you know what? God's going to answer those prayers!

Lord, thank You for the awesome privilege of coming to You and sharing with You the people and things I care about and the problems I have. You are so gracious and understanding. I praise Your holy name. Amen.

Your Priorities Are Showing

※

What do your calendar, "to do" list, weekly commitments, and even your checkbook register say about you? What do they suggest about your walk with God? About your priorities? Take a look. Is it time to line up your priorities based on what you believe and not on the desires and whims formulated by what you see and hear via people and advertising?

Prayerfully consider what changes you need to make to set your priorities on what you believe about God and His call to service. Psalm 90:12 says, "Teach us to number our days, that we may gain a heart of wisdom." A heart of wisdom! That's exactly what you need as you live the priorities you hold dear.

Lord, I'm so easily swayed by advertising and wanting what other people have. Every time I'm ready to spend money, remind me that You are my priority…and that You provide my income so I can serve You, provide for my family, and promote Your kingdom. Amen.

No Matter What!

Welcome to "the adventure of being a wife"! Following a husband is just that. I'm so proud of my daughter Courtney. She's married to a Navy man so she's always on the move as he gets reassigned. She cheerfully cleans out drawers and closets, stops her newspaper, and changes her magazine subscriptions—again and again. She never allows her "nesting instinct" to hinder her from walking away from comfort and security toward something greater…to a life of deeper faith. She trusts God to guide her husband and to provide everything she and her family need. The bottom line is that oftentimes living for God is all about following someone else by faith. No matter what!

Lord, following someone…anyone…is hard. Help me have a discerning heart so I can bend to the authorities You place over me. Guide them and give them Your wisdom so they will wisely handle the responsibility You give to them. Amen.

Life's Often Unfair

Are you feeling like life is unfair? Let me encourage you. When I think of the women of great faith I know, I can almost always point to some sorrow or tragedy that's caused them to have a growing trust in God. A widow who lost her young husband, a writer who writes from her bed because of a disease she'll never get over, a mother who lost a child in a tragic accident, a woman who suffers with cancer.

What's lacking in your life, my friend? I know what's lacking in mine. But I'm giving praise to God for His unfailing loving-kindness and all-sufficient grace. It's what keeps me sane and happy and healthy. And it will do the same for you!

Lord, I don't understand why people have to endure hardships and tragedies. Sometimes I get scared thinking about what could happen. But You are here for me. You will give me the strength and courage I need to persevere. Thank You. Amen.

Home Is Where the Heart Is

※

"Home is where the heart is!" It's so true. Home isn't a physical dwelling. I've seen women who've given up family and friends—to say nothing of homes and beautiful things—to follow their husbands to faraway places. And when I was in South Africa, I saw women who pray each day for physical safety for their families. These women never go out alone because it isn't safe. But each one of these women is "at home" in her heart. They are at home in the center of God's will.

Is there anything God is calling you to that you're refusing today? Joy will be yours as you cling to His promise to uphold you with His hand and take a step in faith.

Lord, search my heart. Cleanse me from any self-ish desires or fears that keep me from serving You completely. My true home is in Your embrace. What an awesome thought! Amen.

Prayer for Patience

Contrary to the adage, "Don't pray for patience because God will give you situations that require it," asking for patience is a good thing! These uplifting words in Romans 8:28 tell us we can "know that all things work together for good to those who love God." God is in control of everything—even those situations that appear negative. And He will work those out for your good and for His purposes. So don't be afraid to pray for patience. God will see you through…and you'll acquire this wonderful fruit of the Spirit!

I love the greeting card that says, "Bloom where you're planted!" As God cultivates your soil, adds growth enhancers, plants, and prunes unnecessary branches, rejoice. Someday you'll say with confidence, "Sure enough, God worked all things together for His good purposes!"

Father, patience is a virtue, I know. Help me nurture this trait so I can better reflect You and wait on Your timing. Thank You for willingly taking the time to develop my character so I can better serve You. Amen.

W-A-I-T

How many times have you heard, "You have to wait." Sometimes God tells us to wait too. Here's an acrostic on that all-important word "W A I T." I hope it helps you as it does me.

W hat benefit will result if you wait?
A lways see waiting as an opportunity to trust God.
I nclude prayer in your daily waiting.
T ime is not an obstacle to God.

W-A-I-T! If you're like me, your tendency is to want everything now. After all, we live in an instant society. But if you want to be a woman after God's own heart, let Him set the pace.

Lord, I get so impatient. I don't want to wait for anybody…and sometimes that includes You. Please forgive me for that. Help me look to You in everything I do and give me patience to wait on Your leading. Amen.

You're Somebody

❧

"It isn't fair! I've done everything I can possibly do. No one appreciates me. In fact, just forget it!" Is this where you find yourself today? Do you think nobody cares? That nobody knows of your suffering? That nobody is aware of you? Take heart, my friend—God cares! And that makes you a very important somebody! God sees. God hears. God notices. And God acts. I don't know about you, but that's great news to my heart! Remember when God came looking for Adam and Eve (Genesis 3:9)? He came looking for David (1 Samuel 16:12). He came looking for Saul of Tarsus (Acts 9). Luke 19:10 says, "The Son of Man has come to seek and to save that which was lost." That means God is looking for you too!

Lord, thank You for caring for me so much and always watching over me. When I feel as if no one understands what I'm feeling, help me remember that You know exactly what I'm going through. Amen.

When We're Asked to Pray

❀

Are you praying for your friends? Really praying? I have to say, not much in life compares in importance—or in emotion—to what's going on in the lives of the people I love. When my father was dying from cancer, I cared very little about world news, the latest books, or anything else for that matter. Somehow things like that don't matter in times of crises. Being followers of Jesus means listening to people and then praying diligently for them. Who are the family members you regularly bring before God in prayer? Who are the friends? Paul's words to the Philippians echo in us too: "I have you in my heart" (Philippians 1:7). Lift a prayer for your family and friends today.

Lord, when You walked on the earth and people brought their sick or paralyzed friends to You, You healed them. Help me to always bring my friends and family members to You in prayer. Amen.

Take a Good Look

❦

"Hmmm, a little tuck here, a little Botox there. Yes, you're lookin' good!" A look in the mirror is often revealing and sobering. As women we check our looks in the mirror, but more important is what's going on in our hearts. How're you doing? If you can say great or even okay, thank God for His marvelous grace. If you're having a hard time, feeling negative emotions, and making questionable decisions, turn from the behaviors that are causing you to fall. We can all use improvement—a little tuck here and there. Take to heart Psalm 1:2: "His delight is in the law of the Lord, and in His law he meditates day and night." Focusing on God will give you the confidence, reassurance, and strength to overcome any hardships and continue in the Lord.

Lord, whenever I look in the mirror, help me also to look at my heart. Please show me any blemishes that mar my spirit. Teach me to live in a way that keeps my soul fresh and clean. Amen.

Waiting, Wondering, Wandering

❦

"Did we get the house? Why haven't they called? Don't they know how anxious we are?" Waiting, wondering, wandering. That pretty much sums my life up! Waiting for a doctor's appointment when I sensed something was wrong. Wondering when God was going to do something about a person or a decision. And wandering as a missionary, living in nine different places in one year.

What are you waiting for? And are you having some doubts? Let me encourage you as one woman to another. While you're waiting, be a giving person. Involve yourself in the lives of other people. "Work out" your faith while you "work on" your faith by patiently waiting. And then one day, in God's appointed time and in His unique way, your faith in Him will be made even more real and powerful.

Lord, sometimes I get too focused on the uncertainties in my life. Help me trust You to use every situation to make me more like You. Strengthen me to give loving attention to the people You've put in my life. Amen.

Getting into the Word

❖

Trust me. Just about everything and anything can keep you from getting into God's Word. Maybe it's the little ones underfoot. Or maybe it's your job. There just isn't time to stop before you dash out the door. Or maybe you just never seem to get around to it! What are your greatest obstacles to spending time alone with God? Sit down and write out what you can—and will—do to find a lifestyle pattern that includes Bible study. Talk to friends about their schedules. Find out ways they enjoy God's Word. Make a prayer list. My desire is that you'll develop passion for God's Word. That you will truly be a dedicated and growing follower of Jesus.

Lord, Your Word is such a treasure! I want to hide it in my heart, to let it dwell richly within me, to use it to guide every decision I make. Thank You for speaking to me through the pages of the Bible. Amen.

Words of Kindness

Kind words are short to speak, but their echoes are endless. Dig around in your heart. Expose any problem areas. Do you need to confess and admit to the sin of gossip? Do this each and every time you do it. Are you dealing with hatred? Foolishness? Idleness? Be honest. As women, let's make godly speech a lifetime goal. We want to follow in the footsteps of Jesus, whose lips spoke words of love and kindness. Let's make this our constant prayer as it was David's—"I will guard my ways, lest I sin with my tongue" (Psalm 39:1). How wonderful to aspire to godly speech! In fact it's our mandate if we're going to truly follow God.

Lord, may my speech always be gracious. Help me not to let any unwholesome talk come out of my mouth, but only what is helpful for building others up according to their needs. Amen.

73

The Older Woman

❧

"This is one of those times when I miss Mom. She would know exactly what to do!" If you're an older woman and you're wondering what to do with your life—you've come to the right place! Who are those younger women in your church you could teach and encourage? Are you doing it? Or at least preparing to? What about the women in your family? Your daughters? Daughters-in-law? Granddaughters? Nieces? When you have some time today, get out a slip of paper. Make a special prayer list and start praying for each one on it each day. God is eager to use you to encourage, to lead, and to support younger women who are desperately looking for someone just like you…someone willing to reach out with God's love.

Lord, sometimes I wonder if I have much to contribute to younger women. But I trust that You can use me to be a blessing to others. Lead me to the people You want me to encourage. Amen.

Your Husband's Helper

✦

"My wife has brought new meaning to the words, 'Honey do'! It's not nearly as cute as it was when we were first married!" Most wives have to-do lists for their husbands. But have you ever thought of yourself as your husband's helper? Before you panic, let me just say it can start with something as little as a donut! Years ago Jim brought up the idea for our family to stop for donuts on the way to church. I had a list of reasons why it wasn't a good idea, including the fact that donuts aren't all that healthy. Well you guessed it. One Sunday I "submitted." I said nothing! We went to the donut shop and had a great time. In fact, it is now a family tradition when we're all together. Are there areas where you can honor your husband? How about starting this week?

Lord, I need help noticing ways I can be a better helper for my husband. When You show me an opportunity to support and encourage him, please give me the will and strength to follow through. Amen.

75

Love Is a Decision

❖

"Brenda, I think there's another woman. I've suspected it for a long time. And now I think it's too late." Too many women have been in this position. What can you do to prevent it from happening to you? The Bible says love your husband. If you don't, someone else just might. Make the decision to love your spouse. Choose to love him ahead of your children. Give him first place (after God, of course). Colossians 3:23 says, "Whatever you do, do it heartily, as to the Lord." When I first began to grapple with this area, I wrote out my commitment in a letter. And then I prayed that letter every day. In fact I still have that letter more than 25 years later. Ask yourself, "How can I bring greater glory to God through serving my husband?" Then take action. Step out and do it!

Lord, You are the Creator of love. Please show me creative ways to love my husband. I choose today to reaffirm my commitment to him…and to You. Amen.

10 Ways to Love Your Children

There's nothing more important than the value of spending as much time as possible with our children. We have the awesome privilege and joy of loving them and molding them in godly directions. In this brief devotion there are 10 ways to love your children! 1) Teach them and train them. 2) Do not provoke them (Ephesians 6:2). 3) Talk to God about your kids. 4) Talk to them about God. 5) Read up on mothering. 6) Read to them. 7) Teach them to pray. 8) Take care of them. 9) Tell them about Jesus. 10) Do your best to model godliness.

A very wise person said, "If we don't set aside ungodliness today—it'll show up in our children tomorrow."

Lord, I love my children! Help me care for them just as You care for me—consistently, compassionately, and creatively. Amen.

I Believe

Do you remember the little girl from the classic movie *Miracle on 34th Street*? She wanted a special gift so badly she repeated over and over, "I believe, I believe." Take it from me, your mind matters. What you think about, dwell on, entertain in your mind will show up in your behavior. Make a decision each day to focus on the Lord. Memorize Scripture. Spend time praising God. And make this psalm from David your own: "Let the words of my mouth and the meditation of my heart be acceptable in Your sight, O Lord, my strength and my Redeemer" (Psalm 19:14).

Lord, sometimes my mind wanders and my thoughts become negative and pessimistic. I choose today to discipline my mind, focusing on You and Your Word. Help me to do that every day. Amen.

Love Your Neighbor

❧

"I can't say I know her that well. You know how it is. I'm busy. Anyway, she's not my type." Can you relate to this attitude? We can't read very far in the New Testament without discovering that to be a Christian means to love your husband, love your children, and love one another...including your neighbors. Ouch! As children of God, you and I, my friend, are commanded to show the kind of love we see modeled by our heavenly Father. The command is clear in John 15:12: "Love one another as I have loved you." As you spend time in God's Word you're going to find the best instruction there is about what love looks like. And loving your neighbor is definitely part of God's plan.

Lord, I admit that sometimes I don't even notice the hurting people around me. I pray for sensitivity so I can see other people's needs and know how I can help. Amen.

Committed to Love

Have you ever done or said or implied that your love for your husband is conditional or even waning? Loving your husband is a 24-hours-a-day job. Scripture says simply, "God is love" (1 John 4:8 and 16). And since we have God in us, His love is in us. That's what enables you to love when you don't feel like it. To serve when you'd rather be served. True, sacrificial love comes only from God. "God so loved the world that He gave His only begotten Son" (John 3:16). Jesus didn't come to be served but to serve (Mark 10:45). It was on purpose, it was deliberate that He died for you and me on the cross (Luke 22; Romans 14:8-9). Ask Him to fill you with strong, steadfast, lasting love for your husband.

Lord, on my own I can't even begin to love my husband as consistently and sacrificially as You want me to. Fill me to overflowing with Your love every day so I can serve from a full heart and never run dry. Amen.

I Can Do This

"I can't do this! And you can't expect me to. It's way more than I bargained for!" When I'm facing difficult or painful times, I pray: "God, Your Word says I can do all things—including handling this—through Christ who strengthens me. By Your grace, I can do this. Thank You for enabling me to meet the challenge!" (Philippians 4:13). Don't get me wrong. I'm no spiritual giant. I'm just a woman who wants God to enable her to meet the challenges of life head-on. With this prayer I'm acknowledging the incredible resources I have in the Lord. It allows me to march right through what lies before me…to truly follow Jesus. My prayer is that you'll not give in or give up. By His grace!

Lord, my resources are so limited. I often feel small and weak. But You are strong! Thank You for giving me the power I need to accomplish everything You ask me to do. Amen.

Mrs. Temper

❀

"Her temper is something else. When she gets mad—Whoa!—just stand back!" If this describes you, God's Word has something to say that you need to hear. Proverbs says a godly woman knows how to wait (Proverbs 20:22). She actually restrains her spirit (Proverbs 10:19). I know what I'm talking about. Meet Mrs. Temper! Actually former Mrs. Temper. I started down the path of mastering my temper by creating a "resolutions" page in my prayer journal. I'm a list-maker, and so I wrote down my sins and held them up to God daily. One unbeautiful habit on the list read, "Stop screaming at the children." I think you get the picture. I love Proverbs 15:28. It says, "The godly think before speaking" (NLT). As my kids used to say, "Well duh, Mom!"

Lord, whenever I'm tempted to say something I shouldn't, please help me whisper Your name instead. Everything looks different when I view my circumstances from Your perspective. Amen.

True Joy

❀

"I thought once I became a Christian I'd be happy. But this isn't working for me!" Our lives are filled with disappointments, crises, afflictions, and struggles. But there's good news. God can give us all the joy we need. True spiritual joy is not necessarily happiness. Happiness comes and goes depending on our circumstances. If all's well, we're happy. But as soon as things get hectic or there's a tragedy, happiness becomes very elusive. God's joy is a gift of grace for the hardships and the problems of life. It's supernatural joy. And it's not dependent on circumstances because it's based on God's never-changing, unconditional love for us. We need to look beyond the hard times and know that all is well between us and the Lord.

Lord, even my most difficult situations can't take away the joy You give me—if only I will look to You. Thank You that Your joy gives me strength. Amen.

The Trusted Wife

❧

"It's not going to be easy to win back his trust. I really messed up!" Proverbs 31:11 says this about a wife, "The heart of her husband safely trusts her." The first time I read that it blew me away! Your calling as a woman after God's own heart is to live life in such a solid way that your husband can build his life on the cornerstone of your loyalty. He doesn't have to worry about your character or how you spend your time. He can feel confident and encouraged because he trusts you. There's no better way to strengthen your marriage than to be a virtuous woman. Imagine! You have a calling to work together with God to comfort and support your mate. What an incredible privilege and ministry.

Lord, I want to be a trustworthy person, but I often feel so weak. I trust You to empower me every day to be the wife my husband needs—a partner he can always count on, by Your grace. Amen.

Money Managing

❋

"That was the bank. We're overdrawn again!" That was my Jim talking to me! I was a carefree, uninformed wife who threw up her hands and said, "Oh, I don't know anything about money. I let Jim take care of all of that." That might sound like the epitome of trust, but that attitude actually represented ignorance, foolishness, and immaturity. If you understand financial matters, find ways to contribute. Take some of the load off your husband. I finally decided to be more active in this area, so I talked to Jim, solicited advice from knowledgeable people, and read books on basic accounting. I encourage you to bone up on money management. Start some kind of record-keeping system. I know this isn't very glamorous, but your contribution in the financial arena develops virtue, character, godliness, and yes, spiritual beauty.

Lord, You call us to be good stewards, and I want to do my part. Give my husband and me wisdom as we make financial decisions together. Show us how to please You with the resources You give us. Amen.

Look to God

❁

What trial is causing you the greatest grief, the sharpest pain, the deepest sorrow today? Is it an unbelieving husband? The loss of a job? The breakup of your marriage? A prodigal child? Loneliness? Whatever your greatest trial, let it move you to God. Hebrews 13:15 encourages you to faithfully offer to God the sacrifice of your praise. Do this even if it's through your tears. Jesus gives us the supreme model of joy in the midst of life's dark pain. There was no greater pain than crucifixion on a Roman cross. But the Lord never lost His joy in the relationship He had with His Father. He even endured the cross. Lift your eyes and heart to the Lord today. Give Him your thanks and praise as you seek His help and comfort.

Lord, may every circumstance in my life move me closer to You. Help me lift my eyes off my problems and onto You so I will always rejoice in You. Amen.

Think Differently

❧

"I just can't get over how I feel. It's making me crazy!" Sometimes you have to choose to think and live differently than what was given to you in your past—or even what may be happening today. Dwelling on the negative, on your weaknesses, on your pain is a choice. Instead, let those negatives turn you to God! By making that choice, you're choosing to love God with all your mind just as the Bible commands (Matthew 22:37). The result is good "spiritual mental health," the peace and well-being the Spirit of God gives when we think and act on the truths of God's Word.

And remember John 16:22, a delightful quote from Jesus that offers hope and comfort in the midst of trials: "You now have sorrow; but I will see you again and your heart will rejoice, and your joy no one will take from you."

Lord, when my mind is undisciplined, help me stop the negative, destructive thinking and redirect my attention onto You. May my thoughts glorify You and bring me peace. Amen.

Think on These Things

❀

"I'm doing just fine." When you hear that do you wonder if the person is telling the truth? Have you answered this way when it's not true? I used to hide my pain. My thoughts pulled me down so far that, in private, tears streamed down my cheeks. How did I counter these sorrows? I kept going back to Philippians 4:8: "Whatever things are true...meditate on these things." I contemplated the truth about God's love and the truth about God's promises. They are constant and never fail.

It's not always easy to shift focus from the situation and onto God, to dwell on what is true. But to live a victorious Christian life, you must do what the Word says. God is at work to help you accomplish whatever He's asking you to do. Trust Him.

Lord, You have given me so many wonderful things I can focus my attention on. Help me to delight in the good things You have put in my life. Give me discernment so I can know the truth and cling to it. Amen.

A Loser

❁

When you feel worthless or like a failure, remember you are a child of God! Ephesians 2:10 calls you His workmanship. From one woman to another, I want you to be encouraged that God has a grand plan and purpose for your life. Oh, you may not feel it right now, but God is faithful and always keeps His promises. He says "For I know the thoughts that I think toward you...thoughts of peace and not of evil, to give you a future and a hope. Then you will call upon Me and go and pray to Me, and I will listen to you. And you will seek Me and find Me, when you search for Me with all your heart. I will be found by you, says the LORD" (Jeremiah 29:11-14). Now that's something you can count on!

Lord, help me see myself as You see me. Not more, not less. Just the person You created with a specific plan and purpose all my own. Thank You for hope and the future You have in mind for me. Amen.

Don't Hold Back!

❋

"She must be mad at me considering how she acted at lunch." Have you wondered about people's motives? Here's some good advice: Stop second-guessing other people's ideas about you. I can't begin to tell you the peace I experienced in relationships once I stopped wondering and worrying about what others were thinking.

Rather than looking for fault in things you've said or done, spend that energy learning from God. Proverbs 28:1 is a good place to begin: "The wicked flee when no one pursues, but the righteous are bold as a lion." My paraphrase? "If you haven't done anything wrong, don't act like it." Boldly go forward, not fearing what people will think. This courageous attitude will liberate you to generously and joyously love and serve others. You'll be amazed at the peace you'll feel and the conflicts you avoid by not assuming what other people are thinking.

Lord, when it comes to others and their responses to me, I sometimes imagine things that aren't true. Please help me discern what is real and trust what people say. Amen.

One Common Symptom

❧

"Dear Abby, I suffer from headaches, stomach-aches, my eyes hurt..." Despite what we tell ourselves, most chronic problems have one common symptom— fear. But no matter what's happening in your life, when you walk by God's Spirit you are blessed with peace. Scripture teaches that peace has nothing to do with circumstances. True peace is knowing God is always with you. Psalm 139:7-10 says, "Where can I go from Your Spirit? Or where can I flee from Your presence? If I ascend into heaven, You are there; if I make my bed in hell, behold, You are there. If I take the wings of the morning, and dwell in the uttermost parts of the sea, even there Your hand shall lead me, and Your right hand shall hold me." The key to peace isn't the absence of conflict—it's the presence of God!

Lord, You are the Prince of Peace. When the wind blows and the storms of life come, I run to You and take refuge in Your strong arms. Your Spirit wraps my heart in peace. Amen.

Life's Little Packages

✼

"If I have to answer that phone one more time today—I'm going to scream!" I know you've experienced this. Welcome to the modern world! The phone rings—a lot. I think of it as just one of life's little packages that can sometimes spell trouble. Someone's upset with me. Or the person says something hurtful. Sometimes the caller is reporting something someone else has said. Or I get information that demands a response or a decision. But as the saying goes, Where there are people there are problems. Thank God for the three wonderful "graces" He gives you: patience, kindness, and goodness—all fruits of the Spirit you can read about in Galatians 5:22. Ministering to others means willingly extending those very actions to them…despite how you feel or how tired you are.

Lord, loving others is an extension of loving You. I want to be gracious and kind to those around me. Every day I come to You, the source of life, to be filled so I will bear fruit for myself and to give away. Amen.

Doing Absolutely Nothing

❧

The definition of patience I use for myself is "Patience does nothing." To be even more explicit: Patience is love doing absolutely nothing. When you've been wronged or ill-treated, "do nothing" as your first response. Pretty countercultural and unnatural, right? Instead of reacting and doing something outwardly negative and harmful, inwardly resist in patience. Doing nothing gives you time (even if it's just a second!) to pray, to reflect, and to act in a righteous manner. Will you do it right every time? No. No one is perfect. But here's a helpful hint. This "doing nothing" process is best accomplished while praying, which you can do in your heart.

Lord, waiting can be hard. I often want to do something to rectify a situation without first checking in with You. Remind me again that You work with perfect timing. Waiting on You is the best thing I can do. Amen.

If Only...

❀

"If only I had taken that job. Maybe I'd be able to do some of the things I've always wanted to do." If only...if only...if only. This kind of thinking is counterproductive to say the least. It's time to give that regret up! God calls us to deal with what is now. "If only" thinking usually makes us sad or depressed. It's impossible to change the past—so why live there? Learn from it, yes. See what God is teaching you and remember His faithfulness. And then move on. Acknowledge God's sovereignty over every event of your life—past, present, and future. Thank Him for the opportunities still to come and look for the possibilities He'll bring into your life so you can achieve your dreams. God loves you!

Lord, thank You that I don't have to be haunted by "if only." You guide me to places of amazing possibilities. As I love You and walk with You, I know those moments will be there. Help me be ready for them. Amen.

A Matter of Trust

"God, this isn't the way it was supposed to be!" Like a child who doesn't get what she wants, I've thrown my share of tantrums. After "one of those days" God seemed to say to me, "Elizabeth, this is the way it is. What are you going to do about it?" I was forced to face reality. Because of my unmet expectations, I'd been postponing positive action. I didn't like what I saw, and I didn't do anything to improve the situation. Can you relate?

I encourage you to acknowledge that God oversees all aspects of your life. Your singleness, your marriage, your family, your job…every detail. Part of trusting God is knowing He's in charge and letting Him do His work in your life.

Lord, I call You "Lord" from a willing and grateful heart. Sometimes it seems as if I want to rule my life, but I choose again this day to ask You to take the throne. I lay unmet expectations at Your feet, knowing I can trust You completely with them, whatever the outcome. Amen.

This Is the Day

❄

"Oh no! It can't be time to get up already. Just five more minutes—please, please!"

"This is the day the LORD has made, we will rejoice and be glad in it" (Psalm 118:24). Oh sure, there have been many days when I struggled with this particular psalm. I was overwhelmed by what was facing me. My to-do list was long, my schedule full, and my calendar bulging. And I was sleep deprived. I know you've been there too.

In Matthew 6:34 Jesus speaks to this too-common feeling of being overwhelmed by life. He says, "Don't worry about tomorrow, for tomorrow will bring its own worries. Today's trouble is enough for today." With these words of common sense, Jesus reduces our responsibilities to those of today only. And He knows that with His help we can manage...and even excel!

Lord, some days require a little more coping power. I can't do this in my own strength so I come to You for a new filling of grace, patience, and love. Then I have something to offer others on those weightier days. Amen.

Time Alone with God

❈

"Prayer and quiet time? I'm lucky to get five minutes to myself for a shower every day." I'm so sympathetic! And yet when we don't take time alone with God, we're in danger of losing the very best that people desire from us. In His quiet time alone with God before the sun rose, Jesus acquired focus for the day (Mark 1:35). He let it shape His plans. Take some moments of stillness to discover God's plan for your day. Then by the time your family gets up, the phone rings, or you get into the car you have His direction to guide you. I know it's not easy. And there are days when it just won't happen. But when it does, you'll be there to reap the rewards and be prepared to meet the challenges to come.

Lord, meeting with You at the beginning of my day restores my soul. I love that You love our time together too. Help me make being with You a priority for each new morning. Amen.

Do Good to Your Husband

Make it your goal to do good for your husband. Proverbs 31:12 says that the virtuous wife does her husband "good and not evil all the days of her life." Here are some ABC's that have worked for me. **A**lways contribute positively and spiritually. **B**e kind when you speak of your husband. **C**ontrol your spending. **D**iscipline, raise, and train your children. **E**ncourage your husband's dreams. **F**ollow his leadership. (Yes, you read that correctly!) **G**ive your husband the joy of a happy home. **H**ave a steady, even-keeled nature.

You get the idea. And know that blessings untold await as you follow God's plan and directions, which include having you treat your husband well.

Lord, help me be good to this man in my life. He is such a gift. Help me be aware of his needs and have a heart to meet them. I want to be an oasis in his life so no matter what desert he slogs through out in the world, he finds refreshment when he is with me. Amen.

Give God Everything

❖

"No way! I'm not letting them out of my sight until they're at least 20. Too many bad things can happen." As a mother and a grandmother I understand this attitude about young ones perfectly. I'm fiercely protective when it comes to the people I love. But giving them to God calms my worries. After all, our God is powerful, loving, and able to take care of the people—as well as the things—in our lives.

When you acknowledge His ability, you'll experience His peace. And as wives and moms, we need that! First Peter 5:7 invites us to cast all our anxieties on God, to give Him everything. So turn your loved ones and yourself over to God. Then you can say with confidence and peace, "Okay, God, let's see what's going to happen!"

Lord, it's hard releasing my little ones to a scary outside world. But I know You will be with them. You love them even more than I do. I choose to trust You and Your care for them this day. Amen.

Attitude Helpers

❧

I've been experimenting over the years with what I call my "attitude helpers." In my desire to be and do all God calls me to, this list has helped on more than one occasion. 1) Pray for those you serve and for yourself. 2) Pray specifically about your attitude toward your work. 3) Make a list of verses that encourage you in joy. 4) Do your work unto the Lord. 5) Tackle each task creatively. 6) Be energetic. 7) Look for the benefits—this will lighten your load. 8) Value each day— one step at a time.

How will you live today? How closely will you walk with God? Incorporate these attitude helpers into your life. When you choose to live with a willing, happy heart, you become a source of God-given joy to all!

Lord, my attitude, though seated in my heart, shows up in my face and voice. I pray that both my expressions and tone will reflect that You are my Lord today and I joyfully obey and follow You. Amen.

100

Your Home

❧

Here's a word to the wise: Make home a priority. Cherish time in your home with the ones you love. Your family—not your career, your hobby, your ministry, even your friends—is to be a top priority. Without love, according to 1 Corinthians 13:2, we're nothing. And I might add that without love we'll want to do nothing. So pray. Ask God to reveal and heal any area in your heart that keeps you from loving your roles as wife, mother, daughter, sister, and aunt. Realize the importance of keeping your home safe and warm— a haven for your family. It's going to take some effort and certainly time, but God's call on your life is filled with great blessings.

Lord, thank You for my home. I want to love those I live with and make them feel honored and cherished. Please make our home a haven. Help me follow Your lead to make these things happen daily. Amen.

Early to Bed, Early to Rise

If you're always running behind, why not cultivate the discipline of getting up early? Do I hear a groan? Well, I'm not a morning person either. Figure out what time you want to have things completed in your planning, in your prep for the day, and then work backward. That's the time you need to get up. And as you turn out the light tonight, center your thoughts on what you desire to accomplish for the Lord. Think of all the life you are "buying back" by getting up early. The time you spend praying and planning in the early part of the day gives you a master plan that works. Up and at 'em! Approach your day with energy and enthusiasm.

Lord, I love our time together, and I want to make a place for it early in the day. That will help me redeem other aspects of my day more fully. Thank You for the strength and wisdom You give me each day. Amen.

Serve Creatively

❦

"I can't believe anyone would think of it! Can you believe we had a picnic right here in the hospital!" You'll be surprised by the opportunities God gives you to creatively show your love. Edith Schaeffer calls it "hidden art." And if you're organizing a home, a husband, and children, you're probably already being creative. My friend Kris buys her children's clothes at the Ninety-Nine Cent Store. With a glue gun, some buttons, and a few leftover "pretty things" she transforms her children's clothing into delightful creations for next to nothing. Eventually she expanded and sold clothes at craft fairs. And now she has a creative business out of her home. All the necessary ingredients were there—a focus on her family, loving provision, dutiful service, and a spark of innovation.

Lord, You are the Creator of creativity. I pray You would give me gifts of inspiration and opportunity so I may delight and bless others. Amen.

Getting the Job Done

❀

I smile when I think about a housekeeping survey I conducted. I asked 100 women, "What keeps you from getting your housework done?" Their answers? Poor use of time. Lack of motivation. Failure to plan. And plain ol' procrastination. Sounds right, doesn't it! When I had no goals—or unclear ones—I was unmotivated.

But now I've changed, although I still fall back into old habits every once in a while. After an in-depth study of the Proverbs 31 woman, I decided to put her virtues into action in my life. She knew her goals and was aware she was on assignment from God to build a home. That's great motivation! She worked hard and was focused so God used her mightily. Whew!

Join me in seeking to become a better servant to God and the people I love!

Lord, it's so easy to focus on myself. Help me overcome that. Great joy can be found in loving and serving others. I want to excel in those things as I seek daily to please You. Amen.

A Faithful Friend

When my college roommate Jan became a Christian, she wanted to tell me, a best friend, all about it. But all I did was ridicule and laugh at her. But she took to heart 2 Timothy 2:24, which reminded her to be kind to all, be ready to share truth, and be patient when wronged. Jan was faithful to God and a faithful friend to me. However, I gave up on her when she changed because of her new identity in Christ. We hadn't talked in a decade when, miles away, I suddenly and dramatically became a Christian. I wanted to tell her right away. I wanted to ask her forgiveness. I called her and we had a wonderful heart-to-heart time. Today we share in the things of the Lord. I'm so grateful to her and to God!

Lord, thank You for the people You put in my life. They inspire me, encourage me, challenge me, forgive me, and love me. Please enable me to be there for others in the same way. Amen.

Touching a Life

❧

"Debbie for chairperson? What were you thinking?" We've all heard such negative comments. Have you ever wondered what people are saying about you? What it's like to be on a committee with you? I have to say that how I might negatively relate to others is my worst nightmare. I ponder, What is it really like to work with me on a project? Am I kind? Am I thoughtful? Do I allow people to share their burdens with me? Jesus makes my life easier, and by following Him and growing spiritually, I hope I make life more fulfilling for others. This begins with prayer. I ask God, "How can I serve this person? How can I lift his or her burden?"

Do you look for ways you can help people? What can you do today to touch another life in a positive way? Proverbs 20:12 says, "The hearing ear and the seeing eye, the LORD has made them both."

Lord, open my eyes, ears, and heart to those around me. Let me be a conduit of Your love to them. Show me how to lift their burdens. Amen.

Night Work

❧

What do you do in the evenings? Do you watch TV? Surf the Internet? I encourage you to make your evenings and weekends count. I shudder to think what I'd be doing (or not doing!) if I'd continued to throw away God's gift of evenings. One Sunday at church I walked right past a friend of mine. She'd lost 40 pounds so I didn't recognize her. She grabbed my arm to get my attention. She told me she'd set a goal to find a new, uplifting activity she could do in the evenings. So she started exercising every night after work. And what a payoff! I was inspired to make my evenings more productive. I encourage you to whisper a prayer to God, asking Him to guide your heart and hands toward a little diligent night work.

Lord, between the end of the afternoon and before I lay my head down on my pillow, I want the hours to count for something. Thank You for the evenings. Help me use this time in a way that pleases You. Amen.

A Good-Hearted Woman

❧

"Sure! How much can we give? And don't hesitate to call us back. This is our kind of project!" How often have you heard this response when asking for help? Okay, so maybe I'm living in la-la land. As Christians, let's always err on the side of sharing liberally. Evangelist Billy Graham proudly said of his wife, Ruth, "She manages the fiscal affairs of the household with more generosity than precision." How wonderful to have such a kind and thoughtful heart!

Have you heard this expression? "Love has hands to help others, feet to hasten to the poor and needy, eyes to see misery and want, and ears to hear the sighs and sorrow of men, women, and children." My prayer for you and for me is that we'll sincerely desire and ask God to help us be generous, helpful, and loving in everything we do.

Lord, I want to have a heart for giving. I desire to look outward to serve You and others. Help me see opportunities to meet people's needs with the resources You provide, giving all the glory and thanks to You. Amen.

Two Are Better Than One

✤

One reason your husband can more readily succeed in his position of influence is because he has no worries at home. Remember the Proverbs 31 woman? By virtue of her character and her ability to manage the home, her husband was able to serve his community in a position of great influence. How can you best help your husband? Appreciate him and encourage him. Take care of your marriage. (Yes, it takes work.) Take care of your family, your home, and yourself. Support your man's dreams. Realize your behavior is a reflection on him. The husband of the Proverbs 31 woman was "known at the gates," he was respected in the town (verse 23). This was in great part due to his supportive, loving, diligent wife!

Lord, thank You for allowing me to be my husband's wife. I pray I can bless my marriage by being the best wife I can be to this man. Help me to complement him in ways I know and those I have yet to discover. Amen.

Getting a Handle on Goodness

❁

If you want to be known as a woman who loves God and serves others, it starts with a goodness that's only possible through God's grace. One Bible teacher describes goodness as "the sum of all God's attributes." Wouldn't it be great if people walked out their doors every day ready to do good…even looking for chances to do so? Goodness takes the step from intentions to active serving. The Bible says, "Therefore, as we have opportunity, let us do good to all, especially to those who are of the household of faith" (Galatians 6:10). Dear friend, look for ways to bless people. Humble yourself in prayer as you seek ways to serve. Shine forth God's glory as you bear the fruit of goodness (Galatians 5:22).

> *Lord, goodness is a fruit of the Spirit. Help me reap a great harvest of this crop in my life. I know it will benefit me, but it will also touch other lives with a bit of heaven. Thank You for Your goodness. Amen.*

A Daily Miracle

Where does today find you? What are the circumstances of your life? What fires are purifying your faith? Whatever your circumstances, God is calling you to live one day at a time. Whether your trial is physical, emotional, or a combination, you'll find a daily miracle as God meets you where you are. He will give you the strength you need when you need it.

You and I have both lived through challenging times. Do you know more about waiting, suffering, trusting, and persevering than you used to? Are you stronger in your faith—in your trust in God? This growth makes you much more effective in living your life and helping others. By God's grace you can do both with joy…one day at a time.

Lord, sometimes I grow weary of the fire and long to stay a little pot of ore. But a pot of ore doesn't reflect Your image. When You look at me, I pray Your reflection shines. Though they're hard to endure, thank You for those times that make such a reflection possible. Amen.

A Woman of Focus

"I'm going to say no. It's a wonderful project, but just not where I'm going with my life right now." Can you imagine yourself saying this? When you have a sense of God's call on your life, you're focused. You know where you're going. You have direction. And believe me, it makes it a lot easier to make decisions. If you don't sense this strong call, rivet your attention to God's Word. Ask God to show you what He has for you to do. When He answers, you'll find it is much easier to say no to "opportunities" that don't fit your priorities or time constraints. You'll also have more time and energy to commit to the options that are right for you. Make all you do count for the Lord.

Lord, I pray that I would look neither right nor left when I'm following You. I don't want to be distracted, even by good things. I want to save my time and energy for the best things You are calling me to. Amen.

Life Is a Race

❈

Life is a race! And by God's grace run it for and with Him. To stay on course, ask yourself: Am I focusing my efforts toward the prize that awaits at the end? Or am I too content watching other people's efforts? Am I training regularly by working out in the daily disciplines of the Christian life? Am I receiving God's grace and His strength for this race of life?

Running the race—living for Christ and growing into His image—requires focus and discipline. Hebrews 12:1 and 2 says that to run the race effectively you must look forward and fix your eyes on the goal. Forgetting the past frees us from regret so we can concentrate on what is to come.

Lord, I don't want to be a bystander in the race of life. Help me as I set out on my course. Give me strength for the tasks You've set before me, and help me put aside the past You've already so fully dealt with. Amen.

An Exciting Time with God!

❦

Have you thought about your life's purpose? Take some time by yourself as soon as you can. Close the door and spend 60 uninterrupted minutes with God. I guarantee you won't be the same after this hour with your Lord! After praising Him, pray about His goals for your life. Write them down. Seeing them in black and white will be very motivating. Select from your list the three that are most significant to you. Rank them in order of importance. Now, as you go through the next few days, ponder these goals. Jot down ways you can achieve them, including specific steps to take. You'll discover new dimensions to your life and new energy for God's calling.

Lord, as I commit these minutes to You, please give me Your goals and dreams for my future. What are the good works You've prepared for me? Show me, Lord. I'm willing. Amen.

God Doesn't Make Mistakes

You will experience a lot of mistakes in life. God isn't responsible for any of them! My dear friend, don't fall into the trap of thinking God made a mistake. Or that He wasn't there when you needed Him. The Bible describes God as being perfect in wisdom—and that includes timing.

Where are you in your journey? If these are tough days, I encourage you to acknowledge that God has planned your life…even if you don't feel like it right now. This will help free you from bitterness and resentment and give you hope. Remember, God is the author of every moment of your life!

Lord, I know my times are in Your hands…I just forget occasionally. Remind me that You knew every day that was planned for me before I was born and that You are always with me. Amen.

God Is in the Details

✤

"I think God is interested in the big picture, but the little details? Nah, He's got better things to do." Have you thought this? I have news for you! God is interested in all things, my friend. And that includes the most pressing problem you currently face. Fill in the blank: "My number one problem is _____."

Each day I identify the greatest challenge I face. Then I acknowledge God has promised to work that very thing for good in my life. This process changes my outlook! Romans 8:28 reminds us that God causes all things to work together for good to those who love Him. If you're a bit pessimistic today, look for the good happening—such as ministry opportunities, a promotion, a new job, deeper relationships. As you go forward, remember your powerful, good God and His promise to you.

Lord, here is my life today. I'm going to tell You about all of it, even the hard parts. Please be with me and help me ask You for the things You want to give me. Amen.

Just for Today

❖

Just for today give your life anew to God. Tell Him, "Full speed ahead!" Just for today pour out your love and care for your family. Be "too nice" to everyone you meet. Just for today take your physical strength seriously and exert yourself. Just for today use that brain power God has given you to grow more beautiful in character. Just for today reach out and encourage your best friend in her spiritual journey. Just for today take one small step toward that goal you're trying to achieve. And finally, just for today make the commitment to wake up every day of your life and repeat this pattern.

Lord, just for today I commit every single area of my life to You—every thought, every word, every action. Let this be a day in which I grow more and more into Your image. Amen.

Your Supreme Service

❁

"If I'm going to be successful, it means long hours at the office." Successful at what? The goal to succeed and/or the income from a job can never substitute for your careful watch over family and home. The work you do for your family is meaningful and important. It's your supreme service to God. This isn't necessarily a popular concept in the eyes of an employer or the other women in your workplace. I determined a lot of years ago that my writing and teaching (even though they are ministry) should never be a reason to neglect watching over the ways of my household. Ministering to your family first is a simple concept with powerful, positive results.

Lord, give me a heavenly perspective on my life today. Help me look to the ways of my family and pour myself out for each member. Give me insight into their value, and let me know true joy in serving them. Amen.

How Do You Spell "Love"?

❀

"I haven't had any time since my baby was born" is a common refrain. Be encouraged, Mom! You're doing the work of ministry big time. "Love" is spelled:

T-I-M-E.

A lifetime of time to be exact. Did you know that 50 percent of a child's character and personality development takes place by age three? And our children need our time when they're becoming young adults in junior high and high school. When our kids are even older...adults themselves, they need our time and they're ready to be our friends. Of the woman in Proverbs 31, it says her children rise up to bless her. Parenting is an incredible privilege! Give your children all the time and resources they need to succeed and become the people God created them to be.

Lord, I'm tired...but I'm a mom! Renew my strength as I love the precious gifts You've given me. Give me wisdom to care for them, kindness in my discipline, and love in every minute we're together. Amen.

True Beauty
Never Fades

❁

Beauty fades…and quicker than we like to admit. We live in a culture that reveres youth and beauty. But Proverbs 31:30 tells us that "beauty is fleeting." And charm is beauty's twin sister. Neither one guarantees a happy life. What guides you? What gives you purpose? The key to real beauty—the kind of beauty a woman who loves God has—is God Himself. The last part of Proverbs 31:30 says, "A woman who fears the Lord, she shall be praised."

When your heart trusts in God, when there is a deep commitment to Him, it influences all you do. Your faith in God generates and adorns the beauty of your life.

Lord, I want to be beautiful in Your eyes. I love You more than anything in this world, and I ask You to help me love You even more today. Amen.

Check Your Schedule

❦

Take a look at your schedule. Did you write in time with the Lord? If you're not fully convinced of your need to seek the Lord regularly, you probably won't do it. I just looked at my own schedule. It's packed with a lot of nonessentials, and yet I schedule each one carefully and regularly. But I also set aside time for communing with God. I hope you do too!

Your faith is nurtured and strengthened when you spend sweet minutes reading your Bible and praying. Psalm 29:2 tells you to worship the Lord in the beauty of His holiness. When you do, His beauty becomes your beauty. And your life bears the mark of a woman who loves God.

Lord, forgive me for making trivial things more important than meeting You in quiet places. Help me remember the times we've shared and encourage me to plan those times intentionally and often. Amen.

Be Faithful

✼

Faithfulness is a major distinction of a Christian woman, and it's a quality God is looking for (1 Timothy 3:11). A godly woman comes through...no matter what. She offers no excuses because she delivers the goods. She keeps her word. She shows up early and sticks to her commitments. She doesn't neglect worship, and she's devoted to duty. Does that sound too hard to follow? Ask God to cultivate His faithfulness in your life.

Now take a quick inventory of your life. What areas do you excel in? What areas do you need to improve in? Lift your heart and desire before the Lord, praising Him for His faithfulness to you, and promising to be more faithful to Him. As the saying goes, You may depend on the Lord, but can He depend on you?

Lord, I have so much to be thankful for...and faithful over. I see areas that I've given to You...and I rejoice with You in those. But then there are those other areas... Help me to press on as I grow in You. Amen.

God's Three-Step Plan

❧

Tiredness heads my personal list of struggles. Can you identify? Tiredness says, "I can't do it." It moans, "I can't get up." "I can't make it to church." "I can't run these errands." "I can't study." "I'm just too tired." The wonderful news is that God's Word says you can do all things through Christ who strengthens you (Philippians 4:13). But you need to follow the three-step plan: Look to God for His promised strength. Rise up and follow His leading. And do it! It's your heart, but God's strength will transform it. It's God's strength, but your will submitting to Him. It's God's will filling and influencing your will. And the result? His fruit will appear in your life more abundantly!

Lord, it's hard to move forward when I just want to take a nap! I look to You for Your strength. Help! Take my heart and my will and make them Yours as I get up and get going right now. Amen.

When Life Is Ho-Hum

✦

"Just spell my life H-o H-u-m!" That was me. An average woman with an average marriage, two average preschool daughters, and an average house. Talk about ordinary. One average-but-desperate morning I shook my fist and cried, "There has to be more to life than this!" My lack of purpose went from boredom, to doubt, and then to rage. God used my search to help me recognize I needed Jesus Christ. I became a Christian not long afterward. Suddenly I saw the purpose of everything in my life. And now I have constant hope, even when the "ho hums" bog me down. God doesn't ask me to understand life's twists and turns. He asks only that I trust Him. And that's what He's asking of you too.

Lord, You give me hope because You created me for Your own purposes. I don't understand everything I'm going through, but I'm so thankful that I'm going through it with You. I trust You. Amen.

Delight Yourself in the Lord

❋

I'm sure to God we sound like children at times, always saying, "I want, I want, I want…" Psalm 37:4 says, "Delight yourself also in the LORD, and He shall give you the desires of your heart." The fascinating thing is that God puts into our hearts the desires we find there. Our plans agree with His plans because they are His plans. You won't know where one leaves off and the other begins. To delight yourself in the Lord suggests you are loving God with your whole being. God, His Word, and His ways are the focus and foundation of your life. His plans are becoming your plans and your plans are becoming His. Isn't that wonderful?

Lord, I love You. Sometimes I'm so amazed by You that all I can do is sit in wonder and worship. Thank You for living inside me and for changing me into Your image day by day. Thank You for giving me Your thoughts. Amen.

More Like Him

❀

Have you ever noticed that the more you are with someone, the more you become like that person? If you've been married a while, you'll notice you and your husband use the same figures of speech. You share many of the same opinions and perspectives on life. You'll even see this principle at work in your children. And if you're single, you experience the same thing with your close friends and family. And it works the same way when it comes to God! The more time you spend reading the Bible, the more you resemble Him. You begin to think as God thinks and do what He would do. You desire what He desires. As you spend time with Him, your life takes in and reflects more and more of His love and glory. Commune with Him each day and spend time in His Word. You'll reap tremendous rewards!

Lord, I know You are with me always, but the special times we spend together are so life-giving. Thank You for Your Word and the light it gives on my journey. Amen.

Majoring on the Minors

So many people today have problems because they don't have a positive relationship with God. They get caught up in the day-to-day struggles and forget to look at the big picture. They major on the minors. What really counts in the Christian life is knowing God. This is foundational.

Sadly we too often focus on meeting needs, providing support, and facilitating fellowship rather than promoting the God who gives us life and loves us so much. John 3:16-17 reminds us, "For God so loved the world that He gave His only begotten Son, that whoever believes in Him should not perish but have everlasting life. For God did not send His Son into the world to condemn the world, but that the world through Him might be saved." Don't forget to offer people the ultimate solution for their troubles!

Lord, help me turn to You first when I am struggling with a problem. Thank You that You always care for me. Remind me often that You have more for my life than only me. Amen.

Try a Little Harder?

❧

"Try a little harder!" How many times have I said that to myself? And how many times have I heard that from others? But life isn't about trying harder. Jesus teaches that our do-it-myself efforts aren't the answer. Instead it's so exciting and comforting to know that when you allow God's Spirit to do the work, you'll enjoy a bountiful spiritual harvest. The "fruit" of the Spirit talked about in Galatians 5:22 are love, joy, peace, patience, kindness, goodness, faithfulness, gentleness, and self-control. This fruit has been described as "those gracious habits which the Holy Spirit produces in those of us who love the Lord." What makes your walk with God satisfying and meaningful is bearing fruit that glorifies your Creator and Lord. Then you become a woman after God's heart.

Lord, how I want to be a woman after Your heart! The qualities I long to see in my own life—the fruit of Your Spirit—come from lovingly cultivated ground. Thank You for spending time with me in the garden. Amen.

Nothing Good

※

"Just be good boys and girls today, please?" This may be what we say to children, but the Bible says none of us are capable of doing good—no, not one (Psalm 53:3). The apostle Paul admitted, "I know that nothing good lives in me" (Romans 7:18). It's only as we walk by the Spirit that we show Christ in our lives (Galatians 5:25). Spending time in God's Word, time in prayer, obeying God's commands in the Scripture, and constantly renewing our commitment to Christ are all preparations for greater spiritual growth. Take a few moments today to thank God and praise Him. Commit yourself to walking in His grace. A woman who's fully and wholly consecrated to God will accomplish amazing things!

> *Lord, I'm just like Paul. I see things in myself every day that I don't like and that I'm sure You don't either. Help me walk by Your Spirit minute by minute so I don't satisfy the desires of my flesh. Amen.*

Does God Really Care?

❋

"God forgot about me a long time ago." Dear friend, nothing is further from the truth! I've heard women say, "But God doesn't care about me. He doesn't see how I'm being treated." I've said it myself, "Elizabeth, why don't you just quit now? Why try? Why bother?" Psalm 139:14 is a wonderful reminder that "I am fearfully and wonderfully made." Second Timothy 1:9 says God has a grand plan and purpose for my life. In Romans 8:35 Paul asks, "Who shall separate us from the love of Christ?" Dear friend, love God with all your mind. Do it by thinking true thoughts about yourself. You'll experience the joy and hope of being in close relationship with God through Jesus Christ. It's then you'll see yourself as God does— as His delightful creation.

Lord, sometimes I become so focused on myself that there's no room to see me from Your perspective. Help me turn my eyes to You and believe the things You say are true about me. Amen.

Mind Games

❧

"Oh sure, he says he loves me, but I know what he's really thinking." Don't be guilty of playing mind games and second-guessing motives. It can be disastrous. Consider the principle presented in 1 Corinthians 13: Love thinks no evil and believes all things (verses 5 and 7). We violate these requirements for love every time we question what another person says or guess at his or her reasoning.

So I encourage you to stop analyzing every word people say. Take things at face value. This takes practice, I know! Spend your energy on God's Word, learning what your attitudes and actions should be in every situation. You'll be amazed at how simple and improved life will be.

Lord, I need Your help in taking what people say at face value. I've spent a lot of time second-guessing. I want to walk in freedom, so I commit to learning who You want me to be and then being that woman. Amen.

A Life of Character

"Have the body you've always wanted! We guarantee success in only 30 days." That's the mantra for today, isn't it? Yes, I'm concerned about my looks just like you probably are about yours. But our true goal is to resemble the heart and life of Jesus Christ. Are you thinking, "Easy enough for you to say. You don't know anything about my life." But that doesn't really matter. Our primary focus is to become like Christ, and we do that by studying the Bible. Second Timothy 3:16-17 says, "Scripture is given by inspiration of God, and is profitable for doctrine, for reproof, for correction, for instruction in righteousness, that the [woman] of God may be complete, thoroughly equipped for every good work." Meditate on God's Word. Cultivate a life of solid character by living for God and focusing on serving Him.

Lord, help me know You better today as I read Your Word. And then let me not only know Your Word but put it into action! I want to experience the joy that comes from growing in character. Amen.

Sweet Encouragement

❋

I urge you to share your spiritual journey with other women. A "group" provides you with personal care and interest. The sharing is delightful and uplifting. You'll have sisters-in-Christ who pray for you. You'll be able to exchange experiences. You'll have accountability. And, yes, even some peer pressure. That's not always a bad thing, you know. It helps me get a lot done, frankly. And there's sweet, sweet encouragement as you stimulate one another to greater love and greater works of love. Hebrews 10:24 says, "Let us consider one another in order to stir up love and good works." Growing in Christ is fun…but stretching. My greatest desire for you is that you become a woman who pleases God!

Lord, I love Hebrews 3:13, which says we are to encourage each other every day, as long as it's called "Today." Let me be an encourager to the women You've placed in my life. Amen.

Early Is the Key

✤

Remember when you used to spend the first minutes of your day reading your Bible? I can't begin to tell you how many times I've made that my New Year's resolution. But what a difference in my life when I follow through. The most important thing a busy woman can do is manage her life. And early seems to be the key to effectiveness. The psalmist says, "To you I have cried out, O Lord, and in the morning my prayer comes before You" (Psalm 88:13). How about it? Would you be willing to get up early for five days? Passion for anything—including God's Word—takes sustained involvement over a period of time. I urge you to develop a passion for God's Word!

Lord, getting up a little earlier for five days seems doable. I commit myself to that. But what I really desire is for those five days to build a passion in me to spend five more days with You in the morning. I'll need Your help. Thank You. Amen.

As a Woman Thinks...

"You're always so grouchy." Ouch! That's where the rubber meets the road, isn't it? For years I was a prisoner of my dark moods, of my dark thoughts. I know all too well the frightening ability thoughts have to program our lives. Proverbs 23:7 is right in its message—whatever we think in our hearts, we are. But as I look back, I'm overwhelmed with gratitude to God for His wisdom. He provided help through His Word—the Bible. Words to help me develop a healthier thought life. Words to give me the effectiveness and energy to truly become a woman who reflects God's graciousness and joy. In times of depression and testing, fill your heart with what's true. Choose to love God with all your mind.

Lord, teach me Your truth! Fill me with Your thoughts as I read Your Word. Give me wisdom to understand what the Scriptures mean. Help me seek You with all my mind and never stop seeking You and loving Your Word. Amen.

Proof of Love

❀

You've already put in a long day at work. So who's going to fix dinner, wash the dishes, and do the laundry? Love means that although you're exhausted, you still serve. When you want to sit down and rest, you continue on. Love takes action even when it requires strenuous effort. These actions are proof of love. Jesus said, "This is My commandment, that you love one another as I have loved you....You did not choose Me, but I chose you and appointed you that you should go and bear fruit, and that your fruit should remain" (John 15:12,16). Where has God placed you to show love by your actions? One woman responded, "In the day-by-day, mundane circumstances of life." God's Spirit at work in you will cause the fruit of love to blossom as you do His work.

Remind me today, Father, that You chose me to bear fruit. May I choose to rely on Your Spirit—not on my feelings—and blossom with acts of love...and love that acts. Amen.

Controlling Burnout

I meet many burned-out women whose lives are way out of balance. It may be for legitimate reasons, but often we spend our energy on the wrong things. One answer may be as simple as picking a bedtime hour that will give you the rest you need for your busy life. Examine your priorities. If you're going to even come close to fulfilling your calling from God, you'll need discipline. What actions will you take to energize God's plan for your life today? For this week? This month? This year? For life? My prayer for you is to be a healthy, energetic, busy woman whose desire is to live out God's agenda with passion and purpose.

Lord, some days I do feel tired, even burned out. Show me today where my life is out of balance. I surrender to You my frantic pursuit of self-will. Please renew my heart with Your passion and purpose. Amen.

Loving the Unlovely

❧

Isn't it so much easier to love people who are gracious and mature? Oh, it's a cinch to love the lovely, but what about people who are hateful? Now that presents a challenge. In the Sermon on the Mount Jesus shocked everyone by saying, "I say to you, love your enemies...for [God] makes His sun rise on the evil and on the good, and sends rain on the just and on the unjust" (Matthew 5:44-45). God's love is never deserved—it simply is! And that's the kind of love you and I are to extend to one another—whether people are rude, ungracious, or unlovely. God will give you the grace and the strength you need!

God, You chose to love me regardless of my faults, failures, and sin. You delight in me and direct me to the good actions You've already prepared for my life. I want to reflect You to others today. Amen.

What If?

❧

"What if I don't get the job? And if I do, what if I fail? And if I fail, then what do I do? What if..." What if? That's a question that always generates fear about the future. What if I never get married? What if I lose my job? Questions like these too easily fill your mind and keep you from loving God as He calls you to do. The future is in God's hands. And they are capable, merciful, powerful hands. Nothing will ever happen to you that can't be handled by God's power and grace. As a matter of fact, the future exists only in your imagination. Oh for sure plan for the future... but then leave it in God's hands. Draw close to Him right now—right where you are.

I remember Your words, Lord: "Today is the day of salvation." You want to save me—now. So this moment I give You my future, along with the worry and fear that separate me from You. I want to walk with You. Amen.

Why Worry?

✦

"It's one-thirty and here comes Linda. She's on time today because I told her lunch was at one o'clock." Have your friends ever done this with you? With a little planning, they won't have to trick you anymore. I keep on track by making a "to do" list for everything imaginable. As I prepare and plan, I also pray. I give God everything, beginning with me. Doing this relieves some of the pressure of my day. I have a bookmark in my Bible that reads, "God is ready to assume full responsibility for the life yielded to Him." That's the secret of growing in Him. Of becoming all you can be. As I give God my home, my possessions, my time, I make headway. Try this process!

God, thank You for giving me a mind to use—to prepare and plan with. Right now I give my mind to You so my plans and preparations for today will show I trust You to care for me. Amen.

Sacrificial Love

❦

Love is not the "stuff" you read about in magazines. Far from it! Love is something you do, not just something you feel. Let me encourage you. When you and I go before the Lord in prayer, He'll show us where He'd like us to love more sacrificially. He'll remind us that we're to obey Him as we walk in His steps and love one another—even when we don't feel like it! The Bible says, "Love is patient" and "kind" (1 Corinthians 13:4 NASB). With God's help, we can do this. As we look to God to empower us, pray the prayer of St. Francis of Assisi: "O Divine Master, grant that I may not so much seek to be loved—as to love."

Father, I kneel before You now. Please reveal to the eyes of my heart a little more of the love You demonstrated when You gave Your Son. Help me rest in that love and love others in the same way. Amen.

141

Filled with His Love

❧

"Well if that's what I get for being nice, forget it!" I'm sure you've thought this…and I've been there, done that too. At least in my thoughts. I confess— I have days when my patience runs dry. I have to go back to God so He can fill me again with His love for the people I encounter. Some days I seem to be beating a path back to God minute after minute. Talk about frustrating! And yet that's my desire—to turn to Him to be renewed so I can obey Him. And as He fills me afresh with His love, I find I can share that love with sincerity. That woman who hurt you today? She's someone God wants to show His love to. And He wants to do it through you. What a privilege for you!

Father, I think of the "fountain of water springing up into everlasting life" that Jesus spoke about. I feel as though unloving people have drained me dry of love and patience. Fill me again from Your Spirit. Amen.

A Quality of Joy

❧

Genuine joy—one that's rooted in Jesus Christ—is an expression of godliness. Does that surprise you? That quality of joy is a sure sign of God in your life. And there are some great reasons to be joyful. Maybe these reminders will lift your spirits today. In John 16:22 Jesus says that no one takes your joy away from you. That's great news! And because it's rooted in Christ, your joy is always available. That's why the Bible says you can "rejoice in the Lord always" (Philippians 4:4). Whatever the circumstances of your life, you have immediate access to God—the source of true joy—any time, any place.

"Joy is the quality of life you have when you're with someone who loves you unconditionally." Lord, I'm so glad that's You! I'm glad You are in my life. Help me remember this moment by moment and revel in it. Amen.

Talk, Talk, Talk

❁

"I love my wife—but she's a talker! I don't even have to be in the room." Now that hurts, but it's often true. Sometimes we women talk a thing to death. A young woman went to the great philosopher Socrates for instruction in oratory. (Okay, it was a young man in the real story.) The moment she arrived, she began to speak—and she kept going on and on. When Socrates finally got in a word he said, "Elizabeth, I'll have to charge you a double fee." "A double fee! Why?" The sage replied, "I have to teach you two sciences: How to hold your tongue and then how to use it." Can you relate? "The tongue of the wise uses knowledge rightly, but the mouth of fools pours forth foolishness" (Proverbs 15:2).

Lord, help me be like Mary, who sat at Jesus' feet and listened. Today may I not try to make things happen by the sheer number of my words—rather, may I say what is needed and leave the rest in Your hands. Amen.

A Family Designed by God

❧

My heart grieves when I hear teenagers…or anybody, for that matter…say they hate their families. The family unit was designed by God. So how can you improve your family relationships? One thing is to give your kids the powerful benefit of seeing a healthy marriage. It's a legacy that can't be duplicated. But even if things aren't ideal, you can still bless and instruct your children. Create a pleasant home environment by living out your leadership role as a mother. Colossians 3:23 is such a wonderful passage: "Whatever you do, do it heartily, as to the Lord and not to men." Write that verse down and look at it as you begin your day. And don't forget your most powerful resource of all—prayer.

Father, You came up with the very idea of "family." You've made me Your child out of Your deep love. Please let me have Your attitude toward my own family today. Amen.

The Beautiful Woman

When it comes to work, we're to be willing and able. As I've thought about the qualities of God's beautiful woman described in Proverbs 31, I've decided her mental attitude is the key to the volume of work she accomplishes. And that attitude reveals the commitment of her heart. Without commitment no work gets done. I used to love just reading, brooding, and watching TV. But one evening I heard a Christian woman I admired say, "I don't do anything sedentary." I thought about that for days. Finally I made a pledge to be more active, to keep moving, to always be doing something. After all, Proverbs 14:23 teaches "in all labor there is profit."

God, though You invented the Sabbath for rest, You are always working, even to this very day. Today, help me rest my heart in You so my body can be energized and able for my tasks. Amen.

Keep Your Eyes Open

❁

There are plenty of people around you in need. How can you help? Purchase double groceries and share them with a struggling couple, a single-parent family, or a widow. Clean out your wallet when an offering is taken for a special cause. Prepare a special meal for a woman having chemotherapy. Or pass along your children's clothes to a young family who's short of cash. Stop by and chat for a few minutes with the elderly lady next door. It doesn't take a lot to make a huge difference in someone's life. To reap the blessings that come with a ministry of giving, you've got to keep your ear to the ground and seize opportunities.

Lord, give me new ears for today. And give me eyes that don't look inward at my own concerns but look outward to others—in the same way Your eyes of love looked down on me and saw my need. Amen.

Esther Edwards

In 1703 a devout woman named Esther Edwards gave birth to a son she named Jonathan. From this woman's son would come an amazing line of offspring. More than 400 people have been traced to the Edwards' line, beginning with Esther's renowned theologian son, Jonathan. College presidents and professors. Ministers of the gospel and missionaries. Lawyers, doctors, judges, and authors. What a tribute to this admirable and prayerful mother! God's mandate to you is to faithfully teach your children the life-saving, life-giving truths of Scripture. With Christ in your heart, you begin your own line of godly seed. Pass the gospel to your beloved children. Your godly influence through generations will be as innumerable as the stars and the sand.

I love Your words, God. You said, "Children are a heritage from the Lord." Let me speak and do things today with my children—and the children of others—that will help them show You to the world, now and in the future. Amen.

Leah

❉

The Bible says Jacob "loved Rachel more than Leah" (Genesis 29:30). But the Lord, seeing that Leah was unloved, opened her womb. She conceived and bore a son. Leah's deepest desire was to be loved by her husband. Her human hope was that Jacob would turn his heart toward her as he held his firstborn child. When her hope died after each child was born, Leah turned to prayer. Are you praying, precious friend? Pour out your heart and bring your tears to the cross of Christ. Call upon the Lord and behold His great and mighty answers. Cast your burden on Him... knowing He cares for you and hears your prayers (1 Peter 5:7).

Lord, I acknowledge today that You are my only hope. You are Hope itself. Even though it sometimes seems like there is darkness all around me, I choose to trust You now and hope in You. Amen.

Rebekah

When Rebekah was asked to travel to a faraway place to become the wife of Isaac, her words were, "I will go" (Genesis 24:58). That revealed a lot about her trust in God. "I will go...with a stranger." "I will go... even though I'll probably never see my family again." "I will go...not knowing what's going to happen or if I'll even like Isaac."

Is there an act of faith you are postponing...even if just for a few days? Any decision you are putting off? Any step of faith you are delaying? Every step of faith is a giant step toward the center of God's will. And you'll receive God's abundant blessings.

It seems like You ask a lot of me sometimes, Father—with no visible guarantees. Please teach me about You today and help me trust that You are my promised blessing. Help me move out...toward You! Amen.

Jochebed

❖

Meet Jochebed, one of God's noble women in the Bible (first mentioned by name in Exodus 6:20). She's a picture of faith in action! Jochebed risked her life for her newborn son, Moses. After Pharaoh decreed the death of every male baby born to the Jews, she hid Moses in a waterproof reed basket by the river. In God's providence, Pharaoh's daughter came to the river and found the baby. Needing a nursemaid, she sent Moses' older sister to find one…and she came back with her mother! Jochebed cast her burden—saving her son's life—on God and He responded (Exodus 1:22–2:9)!

What requires a risk of faith in your life? Sending your child off to school? To college? To married life? Trust God and you'll reap the benefits and blessings of your faith.

When I give something to You, Lord, I get something greater back. When I invest myself in You, I receive a return more wonderful than I could have imagined. You designed the universe to operate this way. Today I choose to believe this and act on it. Amen.

A Virtuous Woman

✦

Proverbs 12:4 proclaims, "A virtuous woman is a crown to her husband" (KJV). It was a grand day when Ruth and Boaz, two people who loved God, married one another (Ruth 4:13). The union of this noble man and woman continued a line of descendants who also loved God. Through their marriage a wonderful, godly lineage extended through time. Boaz begat Obed. Obed begat Jesse. Jesse begat David (Ruth 4:21-22). The family tree of Jesus Christ, the Son of David, includes these noble people (Matthew 1:5; Luke 3:31-32).

Thank God for your children and grandchildren if you have them. They are precious treasures, they are stars in your crown. Pray for them fervently. Encourage them in the Lord mightily. Make sure they know about Jesus abundantly. And support their spiritual growth heartily.

God, I'm grateful that You know my needs and provide for me. Help me be an alert provider to my children of those things that will help them grow in You and bear good fruit. Amen.

Seasons of Life

❧

"I noticed Mom could barely hear us at dinner this weekend. Since Dad died she's never been quite the same." I can so identify with this woman. I've walked through several seasons of life myself. My dad died and my mother was institutionalized all within a few months. And yet during those days I also welcomed my first two grandbabies…one month apart!

Like you, I need God's promises for the seasons I'm experiencing as well as those to come. Isn't it wonderful that God's care is unceasing? His love unending? His guidance unfailing? And His presence everlasting? Absolutely! He is with us, dear friend, through every day, every situation, every relationship, every season. What a joy to know we're cared for by such a great God.

You are "the God who is there," Lord. Right now I can't see the end of this season in my life, but because You are here, I can make it through today. Thank You! Amen.

Preparing, Planning, Praying

❁

Whatever the challenge, the task, the trial, or the crisis, God will provide for you, my dear sister in Christ. Philippians 4:19 promises that God will provide what we need. The wonderful fact is that when God commands us to do something, He also enables us to obey! You can discover that truth for yourself. Step out in trust as you walk through your day with the Lord. Not a day will go by without you experiencing His care. Think of it as the "three P's"—preparing, planning, and praying. God will help you meet the emotional, physical, and mental challenges today will bring.

Manna, Father. Every day You provided that food but the children of Israel had to go out of their tents and gather it. Help me, Father, look to You for provision and then step out in trust. Amen.

The Faithful Five

✦

Count me in for a women's support group! I've often enlisted the help of "The Faithful Five." This is a group of women I've had praying friendships with for several years. I phoned them when grandbabies were born, when my dad died, when my mom had to be hospitalized, when Jim was called on active duty in the army, and when a book manuscript was due. By now I hope you know my desire is for you and me to be women after God's own heart. Yes, this goal takes a lot of prayer and accountability. And frankly, I count on the prayer of friends to help me grow. This lifting up is something special just between us girls.

Father, I acknowledge something I often forget— so much of what I need comes through the hands of others. Today, I especially need friends who will intercede for me with You. Help me ask for help! Amen.

Don't Be Anxious

❊

Jesus said, "Do not worry about tomorrow, for tomorrow will worry about its own things" (Matthew 7:34). If your life is uncertain and fraught with difficulties, be encouraged! God isn't asking you to handle your entire life all at once. More often than not your "what if" imaginings about the future turn out altogether differently. I encourage you to concentrate on today. With God's strength and grace, you'll make it. Choose to draw near to the God who loves you, who promises to care for you, and who loves you unconditionally. Let today be the boundary for your fears and emotions. Take life one day at a time. Okay, make it a half-day at a time! Isn't that what being a follower of Jesus is all about?

> *"Worry is a misuse of the imagination." Oh, Father, how those words fit me! So often I fill my imagination with "what ifs." Instead, help me to keep on being filled with the Spirit today so I can walk close to You. Amen.*

156

Forget the Past

❀

The past makes us what we are, but that's no reason to live there. Philippians 3:13-14 is a breakthrough passage of Scripture: "Forgetting what is behind and straining toward what is ahead, I press on toward the goal to win the prize for which God has called me…" (NIV). Poring over the disappointments and failures you experience will make you tired and depressed. And it's definitely a breeding ground for bitterness. Instead, open yourself to God's grace, to the excitement of living today. Reach forward. Press on. Forget about the past. Look to your glorious future with Christ!

Lord, thanks to You, my past is cleansed and taken care of. My present is where You are right now. And my future is with You, and I will see You as You are. This makes me want to get up and get going! To press on! Amen.

Get Over Yourself

❦

The good things you've done in the past can keep you from looking and moving forward. So forget who you were. What's much more important is asking, What am I doing now? God wants you to forget your accomplishments so you'll keep achieving for Him—right now. Present tense. Whether 20 years ago or yesterday, the Bible says the wonderful things you've accomplished or experienced are to be forgotten. Philippians 3:13-14 tells you to forget what's behind and continue on the path of doing what God calls you to do. Chuck Swindoll said to his church staff, "Get a good education. Then get over it." He had his fellow pastors remove diplomas from the walls in their offices and any other objects that promoted them and their achievements. Your past accomplishments mean nothing next to what you're doing for God today.

Lord, thank You for past victories...but even more, thank You for the future victories You have in store for me. Keep my eyes on the prize of doing Your will each day. Amen.

Forgiving Others

❦

As Jesus hung on the cross He prayed, "Father, forgive them; for they do not know what they are doing" (Luke 23:34 NASB). When we fail to forgive others we sentence ourselves to a life of bitterness. Helen Roseveare was a missionary doctor brutally raped while serving in Africa. She forgave those who wronged her and spent 20 more years doing missionary service. Another outstanding woman of faith, Elisabeth Elliot, forgave the men who savagely killed her missionary husband. In fact, she continued in ministry to the very people who killed him. Ask God to shine His light in your darkness. Search out any bitterness and unforgiveness and turn it over to Him. You'll be glad you did.

Lord, help me to be an excellent forgiver...even when it's hard. Show me anyone against whom I've unknowingly held hard feelings. I forgive them just as You have so mercifully forgiven me. Amen.

The Focused Woman

My friend, do you have a sense of God's call on your life? That's what gives you the direction you need. If you're uncertain what it is, ask God to let you know. If you do know what your call is, have you noticed that it's much easier to make decisions when you're focused on what God wants for your life? Once I caught on to that principle, I had more energy than I knew what to do with. It freed me from wandering aimlessly from option to option. If this concept is new to you, please know that God will enable you to serve Him where He's placed you. You can serve with total confidence and energy knowing He's with you always.

Lord, You do have a call for my life. Help me focus daily on doing what will fulfill that calling. Keep me from being distracted by the "good" things I could do that are rivals to the "best" things I can do. Amen.

Sail On

❀

Discouraging voices are loud and persuasive. Most people are willing to give up at the slightest hint of a storm. There's a story I read about Christopher Columbus. Day after day he sailed without seeing land. Again and again his sailors threatened mutiny. They tried to persuade him to turn back, but Columbus refused to listen. Each day he entered into the ship's log two words: "Sailed on." Those are the two words you need to enter into the log of your spiritual journey. As you focus on truly becoming a woman who honors God, He will guide your steps and empower your service to Him. Sail on!

Lord, You are my divine Captain. Each day give me strength to sail in pursuit of Your destiny for me. Thank You for the perfect voyage You have planned. I long to reach the final shore and hear, "Well done, good and faithful servant. Enter into the joy of your Lord." Amen.

Untiring Activity

❦

Without purpose in your life—without goals that energize you to be all God wants you to be—you just "count days." Is that really what you want? Become a woman of untiring activity. God's grace will keep you from being a breathless, harried, frazzled female. I love the promise of Isaiah 40:31: "Those who wait for the LORD will gain new strength; they will mount up with wings like eagles, they will run and not get tired, they will walk and not become weary" (NASB). Living for Christ means going all the way to the end with purpose and enthusiasm. God's in control. Rest in Him.

Lord, I thank You for the promise of new strength, of wings like eagles, and the energy to run and not get tired. When I get tired, remind me gently of Your provision for all the strength I need to go on, full of purpose and enthusiasm. Amen.

Check Those Habits!

What habits or thought patterns are holding you back or slowing you down in your goal to live for Christ? I asked my husband what he had to lay aside in order to effectively serve the Lord. Jim laughed and said, "Television and food!" He knows that excess in these two areas always spells trouble for him. So Jim looks to God to help him be discerning and moderate in those areas. Take your own inventory. What's keeping you from giving your whole heart to this race God has called you to run? When you lay aside the useless, the wasteful, and the meaningless, you'll be free to serve God with all your being. And that's a great thing!

Lord, help me identify those things in my life that must be laid aside. Teach me to be a moderate person, not easily given to excess. May I find the freedom to serve You more effectively as I sharpen my focus on that to which You have called me. Amen.

Contagious Energy

❊

I love women with energy! The secret is knowing that God's great love means everything that happens to you—in the present as well as the past and the future—will be for the good. How could it be otherwise when you're seeking God? To be that kind of woman means you are confident that God watches over every aspect of your life. Your enthusiasm for life is rooted in the knowledge of the God who promises in Romans 8:28 that "all things work together for good to those who love God, to those who are called according to His purpose." Acknowledge God's supreme role in your life. Set your mind on Him. Now that's contagious energy!

Lord, everything that comes into my life has a purpose. My past, my present, my future are all used by You to bring good into my life. Thank You for causing all things in my life to work together for my good. Amen.

164

No Mistake

❧

"I think God slipped up this time." Let's set the record straight before we go any further. God is the author of every moment of your life. Even more specifically, thank Him for working for your good and for your spiritual growth even in the tough times…especially in the tough times! God has a plan for your life, and He's actively working it out through the people, events, and circumstances of your life. There are no mistakes made by God! He's not only present with you, He's superintending everything in your life. Repeat the principle from Romans 8:28 over and over if you need to: God works together all things—the bad, the good, the unexpected—for your good. He is God, and He's in control.

Lord, You are full of wisdom. You never say "Whoops!" or ask "How did that happen?" Like an orchestra conductor, you bring every event in my life into harmony with Your plan. Thank You for caring so much. Amen.

A Lack of Trust

❧

When you start taking matters into your own hands it's clear evidence of not trusting God. Remember, God knows what is going to happen (Psalm 139:16). And He will enable you to cope and grow even in hard times. He literally works good from bad. Remember the story of Joseph? His brothers sold him into slavery, but many years later Joseph was able to help his family. He told his brothers that what they meant for evil, "God meant it for good, in order to bring it about as it is this day, to save many people alive" (Genesis 50:20). It's a truth found in Scripture, and I've seen it at work. Trust the Lord in your trials, and watch as He keeps His promises and uses the situations for His purposes.

Lord, it's hard to be thankful for trials. And yet You use them to bring positive change to my life. Help me see the next trial through eyes of faith. Give me Your peace as You use my trial as a growth opportunity. Amen.

Serious Prioritizing

I often run a check of my entire life. The first thing I do is ask myself, "Is there anything wrong in my relationship with God?" Then I ask the same question about my husband, my children, my home, my personal growth, areas of service to the Lord, and relationships with other people. I write down everything that comes to mind. I follow that with a time of prayer, asking God's forgiveness when I've been disobedient, unloving, and unfaithful. I also ask Him to mold me into a woman He can use, a woman who truly loves Him. This is a very rewarding exercise. Try it! First John 1:9 tells us that whenever we confess our sins like this, God is "faithful and just to forgive us our sins and to cleanse us from all unrighteousness." Hallelujah!

Lord, reveal anything that is wrong in my relationship with You. Forgive my every disobedience, my every unloving thought, and my every unfaithful motivation. Mold me into a woman You can use. Amen.

The Morning Prayer

Begin your day by choosing to follow God's ways all day long. Pray and purpose to do His will every minute. Yes, even with those phone calls you'd rather not take, the meetings you'd rather skip, the meals you'd rather not cook. My "morning prayer" helps keep me alert to God as I go about my day. It sets me up to successfully face the challenges along the way. And you know, it will also help you experience joy and peace as you go through your day. Throughout the day when you feel harried or overbooked, talk to God. You could say, "Please, God, let me respond in Your way. Help me stay calm. Help me know when to speak and when to listen. Help me to help!"

Lord, each day is so full of activity. Please help me keep focused on You throughout the day. I want to face each challenge with Your joy and peace. Keep me calm amid every storm. Amen.

God's Intention

❧

Fanny Crosby, the famous hymn writer, was blind because of a mistake made by her doctor. Yet she believed in God and relied on His calling. Fanny said, "I believe it was God's intention I live my days in physical darkness to be better prepared to sing His praises and incite others to do so." God gave the church wonderful songs from the blind Fanny. She composed marvelous hymns until she died at age 95. She inspired others to greater faith. The next time you sing *All the Way My Savior Leads Me,* remember Fanny Crosby. And look to God for hope. Let Him transform your disability into service for Him.

Lord, I trust You to bring great ability out of my great disability. I am weak in myself, but in You I find strength and power and purpose. Use all that I am in my service to You. Amen.

When Life Zigs and Zags

❀

I have a plan. That's what God tells the Israelites in Jeremiah 29:11. He declares, "I know the plans I have for you...plans for welfare and not for calamity to give you a future and a hope" (NASB). God wants to encourage you in your desire to be a woman after His heart. It's exciting to know He has a plan! I love the popular greeting card that says, "Bloom where you're planted." Your situation may not be ideal, but it is in God's hands. Your life is not out of control. Oh it may seem to zig and zag, but God has promised you "a future and a hope."

Lord, thank You for the specific "future and hope" You have planned for me. As I look around the garden of life, may I have eyes of faith to see how to bloom where You've chosen to plant me. Amen.

An Adventure

❊

Think about God's plan for your life as an adventure. I know that right now your life may seem to be spiraling out of control—and an "adventure" is the last thing you want. I can relate. I've been there too. But this courageous, can-do spirit is a thought process that will change the way you feel. You're in this life with the God of the universe, the Author of your life. Relax, my friend. Know that His direction in your life is for your good despite the ups and downs. God will make you secure instead of disappointed and frustrated. Focus on what's to come, the new challenges to come, and the rewards of serving the Creator.

Lord, help me relax and not worry about the future. You have a divine journey for me. Keep me focused on the adventure of Christian living—and the ultimate reward that comes with serving You faithfully. Amen.

God's Masterpiece

If you're like me, you want results right now! But patience and diligence pay off. One day a huge cube of marble was delivered to Michelangelo's studio. He walked around it, looking at it closely and touching it. Suddenly he grabbed a chisel and swung at the stone, causing chips of marble to fly in every direction. His apprentice yelled above the noise, "What are you doing? You're ruining a perfect piece of marble." Michelangelo answered, "I see an angel in there, and I've got to get him out." Whether this story is true or false, the principle is monumental. God looks at you and says, "I see someone who loves Me and wants to serve Me...a woman I can use to help others. I've got to get her out!" You were made in the image of Christ, and He wants to set you free.

Lord, sometimes I look at my life and see a hunk of raw marble. Thank You that with each blow of Your divine chisel You are releasing the woman of faith You created me to be. Amen.

The Pruning Process

✤

Are you worried you're never going to get your act together? Do you wonder if life will ever go smoothly for you? Hang in there, dear friend. What is that saying? Oh yes! "God isn't finished with me yet." You are a masterpiece in process. Remember the story of Sarah in Genesis? She was impatient, angry, manipulative, unbelieving. Her life with Abraham, Hagar, and Ishmael was constant tension. But God used the failures, time, and even unhappiness to bring her to a mature faith. In fact, you'll find her name in "God's Hall of Faith" as an example to us (Hebrews 11:11). Pruning is always painful, but it gives you an opportunity to love God by trusting He's at work in your life. Take heart. God will bring about the full beauty in you.

Lord, I'd love to see my name next to Sarah, Rahab, and the other believers in Your "Hall of Faith." They overcame tremendous obstacles through faith. Lord, prune me and cause my faith to blossom. Amen.

Goodness Verses

※

I want to share with you two of my "goodness verses." Psalm 84:11 says, "The Lord will give grace and glory; no good thing will He withhold." James 1:17 reveals, "Every good and perfect gift is from above" (NIV). Memorize one or both of these goodness verses so you'll be prepared when life hits you between the eyes—and it will. God will use these scriptures for your comfort and to remind you of His presence. There's security in that, and it makes your faith real in your everyday life. Say this prayer today: "God, help me remember You are the Giver and the Protector." Consider His power and meditate on His promises. You will be blessed.

Lord, help me today to remember You are my Giver and Protector. You will withhold no good thing from me. You will not withhold Yourself from me…and You are indeed perfect goodness. Amen.

Walk with God!

✥

"I'm devastated. All my careful planning gone down the drain. What was the point?" I'm sure you can relate. I certainly can. But I have one word for you—and it's not a popular one: submission. There are going to be times when you're not happy with God's will for your life…frustrating times when you'll find yourself in circumstances you just don't understand. All your careful planning seems to make no difference at all. But when you surrender and submit to God's will, you are respecting His authority (James 4:7-8). You are welcoming His guidance and involvement in your life. There are no two ways about it: Life is often a mystery. But it's one God knows all about. So walk with Him!

Lord, sometimes I see pain or rejection in Your plan for me and I recoil. But Jesus faced these on my behalf when He walked this earth. May my attitude mirror His…not my will, but Yours be done. Amen.

Trust God in the Dark

✤

"Trust God in the dark." Those are the words of beloved author A.W. Tozer. And they're my encouragement to you today. I urge you not to get discouraged as you seek to grow. Trusting God is the perfect wisdom calling you to faith—no matter what. The truth is, you can eagerly exercise your will and faith in God when you know His wisdom stands behind all events, even the ones you don't understand. If you think about it, following God and living for Him is based on having full confidence in Him. Proverbs 16:20 is a great encouragement! "Whoever trusts in the LORD, happy is [she]."

Lord, it's hard to trust in the dark. I want to flip the light switch and see clearly. But You know the future, so I'm putting my faith in You. Help me walk steadily ahead, following Your light. Amen.

A Pivotal Day

❖

Today may be a pivotal day in your life. Maybe the news is about cancer, your husband losing his job, your friend being involved in an accident. Even something positive can be life altering. When God spoke to Mary through the angel Gabriel and told her she'd been chosen to be the mother of Jesus, Mary's life changed completely (Luke 1:26-37). It meant being pregnant before marriage, anguish for her husband-to-be, and trouble in her hometown. But Mary accepted the news from God by saying, "Let it be done to me according to your word" (Luke 1:38). Make that your prayer today.

Lord, I've experienced painful events that changed my life. Surely even those events were part of Your plan for me. Today I declare by faith, "Let Your will be done." And by faith, I'm saying, "Thank You, Lord, for the end result." Amen.

His Unsearchable Ways

"She's so difficult to work with. I just know she's the reason I didn't get that promotion!" A situation very similar to this had me wondering just what God was doing in my life. A woman in authority over me delighted in holding me back. I kept asking, "God, don't You see what's happening?" It seemed so obvious this woman was tripping me up as I tried to serve Him. Every day for eight years I spoke to God and my husband about this pointless situation. Then one morning I read Romans 11:33: "How unsearchable are His judgments!" God used that to touch my heart. Freedom came as I realized I didn't have to know or understand what was going on...because God did. Everything is in God's hands, so everything will be okay.

Lord, I want to see results now, not tomorrow... and certainly not eight years from now! But You do all things in Your perfect timing. Help me wait with patience and anticipation for Your plan to unfold. Amen.

Transforming Your Faith

✤

Dr. Carol Talbot was a missionary in India who underwent nine surgeries over 17 years. She almost gave up her missionary work because of it. But one thing kept her from packing her bags. Every time she wanted to quit, God would bring to her mind a verse she'd memorized. When she tried to dismiss it, God would bring to memory another verse, and then another. Because Carol had memorized so many verses she said, "I was unable to forsake my missionary service. God turned me from a pygmy into a giant." God used her disease to transform her into a woman of strong faith and a giant in His service. When you commit God's Word to memory, He uses it as an instrument of growth—a means to help you persevere and grow strong in Him.

Lord, thank You for Your transforming Word. Oh how it speaks to me when times get tough! In Your Word I find hope and strength. Help me memorize Your Word. And please bring specific scriptures to mind in my times of need. Amen.

A Servant's Heart

❀

Tape this over your kitchen sink or on the refrigerator door or at your desk: "True service is love in working clothes." Jesus said that He "did not come to be served, but to serve" (Mark 10:45). Put on those work clothes of love and serve your husband, your children, your extended family, and your friends. Every meal prepared, every piece of clothing washed, every room tidied, every visit, every act of doing for others is love in action. Married or single, you can exercise your servant heart wherever you are. There are always meals to take to those in need, Sunday school classes to teach, and people to encourage. Ask God to make your heart the heart of a servant.

Lord, cultivate within me a servant's heart. Open my eyes to the opportunities around me to serve others. May my every action for those around me be done with gladness and love. Amen.

A Gracious Woman

❖

You're about to meet one of the most gracious women of all time. Her name is Hannah. We can learn a lot from her. Her name means "gracious, graciousness, grace, and favor." Hannah is one of the few women in the Bible where nothing negative is reported. How did she become such a testimony to God's grace? Answer: Through difficulty, pain, suffering, and sacrifice. Her life had many problems, but it was also filled with fervent worship. The very first chapter of 1 Samuel tells us that Hannah wept much and prayed to the Lord (verse 10). What an amazing role model for us. Her mind was dark with pain but her faith was radiant.

Lord, I am inspired by Hannah's example. Though she struggled with great difficulties, she did not waver. She trusted You with her whole heart. You gave her gracious strength, and I know You can do likewise for me. Amen.

God's Child

Babies don't come with owner's manuals. Even if they did, the guide probably would gloss over the most important aspect of raising children. Training a child for God requires that you love God with all your heart. You can best give away what you have experienced yourself. I encourage you to teach your child God's Word and His ways. Share how the Lord is present and influencing the moment-by-moment unfolding of every day. Acknowledge God's power and His sovereignty in your life and theirs. Emphasize His protection and His compassion. Worship the Lord in your kids' presence. Your devotion to God and His Son points your child to eternal life. Do what you can now to surround your children's lives with the God you love.

Lord, as my heavenly Father, You are intimately involved in every detail of my life. Help me to share about Your goodness with my children and others so they too can see how great You are. Amen.

You Are Not Alone!

❧

Everyone's life is stained with sin. You are not alone in your struggle to live a godly life. But be assured that God loves you. He cares for you. You can count on and enjoy the promise and reality of His forgiveness. Forgiveness! Just the sound of the word brings joy to my heart. In Jeremiah 31:34 God says, "I will forgive their iniquity." In fact, the verse also says that God will remember our sin "no more." Claim that promise today. Now don't brood over the situation and what happened. When you keep going over confessed sin you're doubting God's mercy. This robs you of spiritual progress. Acknowledge your sin before God, receive His cleansing and forgiveness, and then with renewed joy serve Him and love Him wholeheartedly.

Lord, how amazing is Your gift of forgiveness! With it comes freedom from the guilts of the past—a freedom that is real and lasting. May I never take Your forgiveness for granted. Amen.

Speak Up...but Not Always

There's a time to speak...and a time for silence. Knowing when to employ each is often the great challenge. I've struggled with this, and over the years I've had to learn—sometimes the hard way—that speaking and being silent also involve knowing the right timing and the right issues. Proverbs 20:18 reminds us, "By wise counsel wage war." How are you doing in this area? Do you know that when you choose to say something, how you say it is usually more important than what you say? Ask God to show you the right times to speak and the right times to be silent. Be very still while you wait for His answer. Wait patiently... then follow His advice.

Lord, help me speak with discernment. May the words of my mouth be chosen with care, and may I be alert for those times when it is better to stay silent. I pray You will be glorified in everything I say. Amen.

The Heart of a Home

❧

Psalm 128:3 says that a husband's "wife will be like a fruitful vine in the very heart" of his house. What message does God have for you in this lovely word picture of fruit and vine, of heart and home? What can you, a woman who serves God, take from this? You are the center of your home, positioned to give gifts of peace and pleasure to your household. In the hot and sunny land of the Bible, a vine brought protective shade. Like those vines, you have the ministry of sheltering your family. What makes a happy home? At the heart is a content woman, wife, and/or mother who is bearing abundant fruit of love, joy, and faithfulness.

Lord, thank You for entrusting me with such an important role in the home. My heart's desire is to be a fruitful vine that brings blessings to all in my household. Enable me in the way only You can. Amen.

One Happy Fella

❖

"How to Become the Woman of His Dreams!" How many magazine articles have you seen centered around this message? I can't guarantee you'll become your husband's ideal mate in every way, but if you meet God's standards for marriage, that husband of yours will be one happy fella! First, be a woman who fears the Lord. That's where true excellence is grown. Then love the Lord and obey His commands. Stay unshakably faithful to your marriage vows. Be glad when your husband is the center of attention. Cultivate fierce loyalty to him. Keep his shortcomings and failures to yourself. Be a positive emotional influence. Honor your husband daily and for life. Proverbs 12:4 calls that kind of woman "an excellent wife who is the crown of her husband."

Lord, thank You for the reminder that when I aim to fulfill Your design for marriage, I become a more excellent wife. Putting You first helps me put my husband first. May I take to heart what Your Word says to me as a wife. Amen.

A Prudent Woman

❧

Prudent? It sounds so old-fashioned...but what a wonderful attribute for any woman to have. *Prudent* is exactly what Proverbs 19:14 calls the wife who is from the Lord: "Houses and riches are an inheritance from fathers, but a prudent wife is from the LORD." This wife is in a special category. She's a blessing to her husband directly from the hand of God. A husband is set for life with a wife like this. Replace the word *prudent* with *disciplined, reasoned, practical, delightful*...and you begin to get the picture. You are one of the Lord's greatest gifts to your husband!

And you don't have to be married to reap the rewards of being a prudent woman. You'll be blessed... and you'll be a delight to everyone around you.

Lord, teach me to be prudent. Help me exercise diligence, wisdom, and self-control in all I do. Though living prudently requires work on my part, I know the blessings to me and others make it worthwhile. Amen.

A Heart for God

❋

"Why would God use me?" Have you ever wondered this? Consider the choice of Mary as the mother of God's Son. Mary was young and probably not from a prominent or wealthy family. We aren't given any details about her physical appearance or information about her father and mother. We're not told of any outstanding characteristics in Mary except her love for God. This may not be the sole reason she was chosen, but the angel who delivered the news to her said, "Rejoice, highly favored one, the Lord is with you; blessed are you among women!" (Luke 1:28). He continued, "Do not be afraid, Mary, for you have found favor with God" (verse 30). What was Mary's reply? "Behold the maidservant of the Lord! Let it be to me according to your word" (verse 38). And that's what God wants! Hearts of obedience and trust.

Lord, help me remember that in Your eyes it's my heart that counts. I give my life wholly to You so You can do the work You desire to do within me. Amen.

Resting in the Lord

❧

"I'd love to do that for you, but I can't add one more thing to my schedule!" We've all either heard this, said this, or both. We never seem to have enough time, do we? How are you handling the pressures of life? With peace or panic? I liken our lives as women to a "hurricane of female hyperactivity." And that's not always a good thing. The fact is, when we're running around in circles, we're not doing as the Bible says when it calls us to "rest in the LORD" (Psalm 37:7). Is your relationship with Jesus your first priority? Or are you just too busy to sit at His feet and enjoy His presence? The woman whose heart and soul are at rest is the woman who embraces this truth of Scripture: Our times are in God's hands.

Lord, thank You for the gift of time. Help me use it in ways that honor and glorify You. Give me the wisdom to know when to let go of my schedule, concentrate on Your guidance, and help others. Amen.

The Power of a Woman

"Never underestimate the power of a woman!" Old cliché or not, when God is at work in your life—watch out! Acts 16:14 describes just such a woman used by God in the growth of the church at Philippi: "Now a certain woman named Lydia heard us…. The Lord opened her heart to heed the things spoken by Paul." She was a woman faithful in worship. Attentive to prayer. Instrumental in bringing others to the Lord. Paul's message helped her and now she wanted to help him and his friends by opening her home to them. Her hospitality allowed them to do their ministry. Never underestimate the power of a woman, especially when she's serving the Lord. And that includes you!

Lord, I thank You for Lydia's example of what You are able to do through a life surrendered to You. Help me make the right choices about my time and my priorities so You are able to work through me unhindered. Amen.

Singleness

❧

"I was so sure I'd be married with children and living in the suburbs! Where did I go wrong?" Too often Christian circles put too much emphasis on being married and having children. Clearly marriage is not a requirement to be a woman after God's heart. First Corinthians 7:34 says the unmarried woman cares about the things of the Lord. If you are single, you are less distracted because you don't have the responsibilities of being a wife and a mother. You have the opportunity for greater devotion to God. Dear single friend, the chance to be fully committed to God, to serve Him with a no-holds-barred devotion is a gift. Never allow a longing for marriage—or anything else—to rob you of the complete joy and fulfillment God means for you to know each day. Live fully and gloriously unto the Lord!

Lord, no matter what my marital state, may I seek to follow You with all my heart. Only You can fulfill my longings. May I not let the things of this world come between You and me. Amen.

Show Me

✤

"I can't help it! I just know I'll fail, so why bother?" Does that sound like you today? Well, one sure way to face your fears is to equip yourself with the knowledge and assurance that comes from God's Word—from knowing His promises. This reminds me of my junior high algebra teacher who was from Missouri, the "Show Me" state. One of her teaching methods was to say, "Show me!" She wanted proof we knew what we were talking about. So cultivate your knowledge and faith in God's Word. This kind of wisdom and belief allows you to face your fears and show others where your strength and endurance come from. God is calling you to move out, conquer those fears, and share His provision. Can you hear Him? He's saying, "Show Me!"

Lord, You never meant for Your children to live in fear. That's why, in Your Word, You've given promises of strength, protection, and hope. May I take time to hide Your promises in my heart so I will no longer be afraid. Amen.

Bearing Fruit for God

❧

"What does my personal life have to do with it? You're looking for volunteers at church, and I'm available." Actually your personal life has everything to do with how you serve. "Love, joy, peace, patience, kindness, goodness, faithfulness, gentleness, and self-control"—all these aspects of your life mentioned in Galatians 5:22 come when you have a faithful, steady, growing walk with God. Your life is like a watch that contains many parts. Oh, it can be taken apart for cleaning and repair, but each piece must be in place for the watch to run efficiently and correctly. You can enjoy a closer walk with God. You bear much spiritual fruit as you surrender your life to Him. And that's when we truly glorify our Creator and Lord in every aspect of our lives.

Father, help me continue to learn more about You. I want Your love and wisdom to permeate my life... and be passed on to others. Thank You for loving me. Amen.

Search Me, O God

❧

"There's nothing I'd like better than to put him in his place!" Hmmm…which weaknesses are most evident in your life? When was the last time you prayed this prayer of David found in the book of Psalms? "Search me, O God, and know my heart. Try me, and know my anxieties—and see if there is any wicked way in me" (139:23-24). That's where the rubber meets the road, isn't it? Then what do you do? You need to confess what God reveals to you and submit to the transforming power of God's Holy Spirit. This means living each moment in submission to God. We please God with the thoughts we choose to think, the words we choose to say, and the actions we choose to take. Let God work in you today!

Father, I want to pray as David prayed—that You would reveal to me the condition of my heart. Help me be sensitive to Your transforming work within me so that my every thought, word, and action is pleasing to You. Amen.

God's Love "Is"

✽

Have you ever told someone "I'll call you" with no intention of doing so? Okay, maybe you've never said that, but how many times have you thought it? Well, God's love for us wasn't deserved either. And this truth needs to play out in our lives. Luke 6:35 says, "Love your enemies, do good, and lend, hoping for nothing in return; and your reward will be great, and you will be [daughters] of the Most High." Is someone in your life difficult to love? Think about it this way. We're God's children, and we have His love in us. And He commands us to love others. Refusing to do so is like saying, "God, I don't love You enough to love that person." Ouch! My friend, God enables us to love as He loves—everyone, all the time, unconditionally.

*Father, when I see someone who is filthy or smells...
or meet someone who hits a negative chord in me,
remind me I am Your representative on earth.
Give me the strength and grace to love him or her.
Amen.*

No Expectations

❃

When we're nice to someone, we automatically expect that person to be nice to us. And when this doesn't happen, look out! Interestingly, Jesus said to do good, but He also said to expect nothing in return (Luke 6:35). Loving without thought of personal reward can be extremely difficult. In my ministry I often hear, "Elizabeth, I've served my husband faithfully, but he never does anything in return." Is this how you feel? Or is there a friend you're always helping without receiving any thanks? The Bible says, "Through love serve one another" (Galatians 5:13). When you serve someone, you are serving the Lord. That kind of love is never self-seeking. Its only intent is to love as Jesus loved.

Father, may I be more generous with my love, not expecting anything in return. May my satisfaction come from growing to love others as You love them. And may I never take Your love for granted. Amen.

The Good News

❧

"I don't think I can take one more disappointment." Oh, how I identify with that struggle! Real life is filled with disappointments, tragedies, heartaches, and just plain old struggles. And I get tired of it, just like you do. But then I remember the good news. God can give us the joy we need—just when we need it. Jesus wants our joy to "be full." It says so in John 15:11. When we depend on God in the middle of our suffering, we'll find the power we need to praise Him despite the pain. We can actually give thanks for His goodness even when things aren't so good! Thanks to the working of God's Spirit in us, we can become women who love God in every circumstance.

Father, Your Word makes the Good News abundantly clear—I can know joy even when life is difficult. Help me to not become so preoccupied with my problems that I lose sight of the many blessings You continue to bring into my life. Amen.

Fear to the Heart

❦

There's nothing like facing a biopsy, or surgery, or hearing a cancer diagnosis to bring fear to the heart. That kind of danger always stirs up our emotions. But sometimes it's the everyday events of life that cause panic and dread. In all those times we definitely need God's peace. My friend Elisabeth Elliot says, "Trust God. Right up to the fingernail-scraping edge!" I never want to sound like I'm preaching—or that there's a simple answer to what you're going through. We've both heard too often, "Just get over it!" But the truth is, you can trust God. Allow the Holy Spirit to fill you with His peace when you walk through trying times. Lean on Him for comfort and strength.

Father, trials are part of life. Help me remain positive and upbeat as I rest in Your love and trust You to see me through. Thank You for wanting the best for me. Amen.

198

Patience Is a Virtue

❧

Patience is a virtue. Unfortunately, it's not one I'm always able to pull off. But God's Word says, "Put on a heart of patience!" First Timothy 6:11 says, "Pursue righteousness, godliness, faith, love, patience, gentleness." Just as we cover ourselves every day by putting on clothes, we are to dress our spirits with patience. And here's the hard part. When we see faults in other people or when we're annoyed by them in any way and want to be critical and lash out, we're to employ patience. That's an important key to harmony in all relationships. And believe me, sometimes it takes all of God's strength to help me remain silent and do nothing. Can you relate? It takes God's transforming grace for me to be patient in all situations.

Lord, when "patience" comes up I immediately think, "Be careful what you ask for!" because patience is so hard to learn. But Your Word says patience is good. It's a sign of someone who loves and serves and grows in You. And that's me, Lord! Teach me patience. Amen.

Smoothing the Rough Edges

God commands us to be kind. It's as simple as that...but it can be so hard to implement. We all get into debates and have emotions that run hot. Realistically, I can't imagine a home or office that doesn't have moments of tense exchanges. We need to turn our negative energy into God's kind of grace and kindness. How do we begin? Love others more than ourselves. It'll take some practice, but with God's help through prayer, we can make it happen. When we genuinely care about someone, we pay attention. We get involved. And that person becomes more important to us. Will you join me in letting God soften our hearts and smooth our rough edges? He'll make us into women who can be kind and gracious in every situation!

Father, it's so easy for me to get upset when something I've worked on doesn't get done right. It's hard to not be in control 100 percent of the time. In fact, Lord, I'm not in control. You are! Help me remember that. Amen.

My Best Intentions

"Yes! Chocolate cake! I'm wearing my 'large clothes' at the moment. I'll diet tomorrow. And pass me that whipped cream too!" We've all been here, haven't we? The comic strip opossum Pogo said, "We have met the enemy—and it is us!" That's exactly how I feel so many times. I start with such good intentions, but as the day passes I eat all the wrong stuff, hardly put a dent in my "to do" list, and don't set aside time with the Lord. I'm truly my own worst enemy. But our God is a God of faithfulness. And He will not judge our success or failure. He will judge our faithfulness. I so long to hear Jesus say, "Elizabeth, my good and faithful servant" (Matthew 25:21,23).

Lord, You know how I am. I have good intentions but so easily get sidetracked and lost. Thank You for Your gracious mercy. Gently put me back on Your path when I stray. Thank You. Amen.

Rebellion

"He goes his way and I go mine. And that's the way I want it." Is this your attitude toward your husband? Rebellion says, "I won't do what the Bible says. I won't listen to my husband. I won't do what the counselor advised. I won't!" Proverbs 29:1 warns clearly that the person who hardens her neck will suddenly be broken beyond remedy. There's no deadlier attitude of the heart than rebellion—whether it's blatant or subtle, in full view or hidden.

Take your spiritual pulse today. Is there any part of God's Word you are rebelling against? Any godly counsel you are refusing to accept? Ask the Lord to fill your heart with His love and faithfulness so you can be the woman He created you to be…loving, caring, gentle, obedient.

Lord, I confess there are times when I want to do my own thing in my own way. I want to indulge myself and not listen to anyone else. Sometimes I don't even want to listen to You. Be patient with me, Lord. I really do love You! Amen.

A Sense of Security

✦

Think of God's plan for your life as an adventure! This will improve your attitude by giving you a sense of security. God is in charge even when life seems anything but secure. My friend Jerry has the right idea. When he's facing a difficulty, he puts a note in a folder that's labeled, "Wait a week!" And then he prays. At the end of the week he pulls out the paper and prays, "Okay, Lord, what are we going to do?" Jerry is confident that "God is still on the throne." I confess that I'm no Jerry! But I too know God is faithful. And the truth that "God is still on the throne" means nothing can interfere with His plans. What a comfort in this oftentimes crazy journey.

Father, it's a relief to know You're in charge. I don't have to make things "right" or worry about what's happening. You will make all things fit into Your plans. Amen.

When You're Tempted

❀

"It's flattering to have him pay attention to me. It's more than I can say for Brian. And lunch? What can it hurt?" If you're alive, you're tempted. That's a simple fact of life. That's why you and I need God's self-control every minute of every day. We need His help to resist our "urges" regardless of how innocent we'd like to think they are. "No" can be a hard word to say, but it's the key to self-discipline. The psalmist says, "I will set no wicked thing before my eyes" (Psalm 101:3). Pray over everything—your marriage, your work, your trials, your temptations. The good news is that you can claim God's power. You can walk by His Spirit. You can win the battle. Isn't that wonderful!

Father, I'm so thankful You're in my life. "I can resist anything except temptation" seems so true. But in 1 Corinthians 10:13 You promise to not give me more than I can bear without giving me a way of escape. I praise You! Help me do my part. Amen.

Innocent Talk?

❀

Godliness and maliciousness don't go together. That's pretty obvious. But we women often get caught up in behavior that doesn't honor God. I'm talking about gossip. We hear something about someone and pass it on because it's funny, or entertaining, or interesting. We like to be the source of information. But gossip translates to slander, and biblically "slanderer" is used in reference to people such as Judas Iscariot, the man who betrayed Jesus. It's also a title used for Satan. That's not very good company to be in! James notes, "Out of the same mouth proceed blessing and cursing." Then he exclaims, "These things ought not to be so" (James 3:10). Let's make Psalm 19:14 our motto: "Let the words of my mouth and the meditation of my heart be acceptable in Your sight, O LORD!"

Lord, give me wisdom to know when to speak and when to stay silent. I want to honor You and also be a person who constantly uplifts and blesses others. Show me how I can share a kind word or encourage someone this week. Amen.

A Friend of Women

"I could never work for a woman! They're too bossy and full of themselves." I've heard those exact words! And more often than not, it's based on jealousy not truth. Let's be friends of women. Let's be people who find the good in others, who love our "sisters" through Christ. No, I'm not saying, "Women unite! We need to stand together against the world." Not at all. Jesus said that people will know we are His disciples by how we love one another (John 13:34-35). So be ready with a positive phrase or two when your women friends are being maligned. For instance, you can say, "That just couldn't be the case. She's too kind to do something like that."

Father, gossip and criticism are hard habits to break. I like the feeling of being "in the know," of being part of what's happening. But, Lord, I want to serve You and follow Your guidance even more. Help me control what I say and what I hear. Amen.

Stress and Strain

Stress and strain are universal. We have so many responsibilities, roles, relationships, and commitments...some worthy and some not so worthy. Are you ready for some relief? When you and I don't meet with the Lord regularly, we can forget the power and assurance we have in Him. It's true. We're more likely to remain calm when we know what it's like to be still and immersed in the presence of God. We're more likely to restrain from appetites and impulses when we know God provides for our every need (Psalm 23:1). God's Word is alive and powerful! It helps us discern the thoughts and intents of our hearts and align them with God's. So get into the Word regularly. You'll never regret the time you spend with God.

Father, give me a discerning heart when it comes to reading and taking in Your Word. Open my eyes to Your truths and Your wisdom. It's through Your Word that I get the knowledge I need to follow Your path. Amen.

A Woman's High Calling

❧

I'm so blessed to have many older women in my life. But I didn't really know just how blessed I was until I got a letter from a woman who has no one to look up to. No one to teach her and show her the way to godly living. No one to encourage her to pursue God's highest calling. Isn't that sad?

I hope and encourage you to commit your life to becoming one of God's precious "older" women in the Lord. And this applies to anyone spiritually younger than you, be it a year or ten or twenty. To be a teacher that imparts wisdom and encourages others is God's will for your life. It's one of God's highest callings. Share what is excellent, what is good. The person you're mentoring will be blessed…and you'll be blessed!

Father, give me the confidence and outgoing spirit
I need to reach out to others in Your name to share
Your love and wisdom. Show me how to speak and
what to say. Amen.

Portrait of a Mother

At a ministry event a man came up and shared with me. He said, "My mom's done a lot with her life, but I never felt I mattered to her. I've tried to be a good son, but it seems like she still doesn't care about me." Isn't this sad? And in such a contrast to the woman and mother in Proverbs 31. The Proverbs 31 woman is a portrait of a mother loving and teaching her son. And what did she teach this little guy? Morals, leadership principles, and fitting behavior for a godly man. But her lessons went further. She was the model of the gal he was to look for to marry…a godly, loving woman not afraid to serve others. Being moms and teachers takes time away from other things we'd like to do, but what a great privilege to pour our efforts into the lives—and hearts—of our precious, God-given children!

Father, thank You so much for blessing me with my children. Help me bring them up to be lovers of You, to be girls and boys who reflect Your character. Amen.

Do Something Special

❈

"Hi, honey. I'm home!…Honey, are you here? I'm home…" Face it. If you don't pamper that husband of yours—someone else just might! Do something special every day for your man. One woman I know has hot chocolate ready each evening for her hubby. They share delicious cocoa and conversation. My daughter Courtney pampers her husband by keeping homemade chocolate chip cookie dough in her freezer so she can treat him to warm cookies and milk each night when he's home. (Are you sensing a theme?) I know these are little things, but they deliver a loud and yummy message: I love you! Pray for your guy daily. Count the ways you can pamper him. Be the woman of Proverbs 31, who enables her husband to rise to greatness and, in return, is blessed by him and her children.

Father, I get caught up in what the kids are doing, how my career is going, what I need to accomplish. I want to keep my eyes on the priorities You've given me: You, my husband, my family, my friends, and others. Amen.

Time to Regroup

"If you kids don't settle down you're grounded—for life!" I'll never forget the time Jim and I stopped by one of our daughters' houses. She'd given us a key so we wouldn't ring the doorbell in case the kids were asleep. Our daughter was on the couch with her Bible on her lap. The house looked like a tornado hit it! I think I even spotted spaghetti noodles hanging from a light fixture. She looked up and said, "You wouldn't believe what happened around here. The kids were awful. I just had to take a few minutes and ask God to remind me how much I love and wanted these children!"

I was so impressed and pleased. She had the sense to stop, leave things as they were, and look to the Lord for His patience and a quiet spirit. Remember to do that when your life turns topsy-turvy.

Lord, thank You for always being available for the little things and the big things. I love that I can come to You for comfort, strength, and peace. Amen.

Enthusiasm for Jesus

If you're a young mom, this God-ordained time with your children will make a difference—a tremendous difference—in their lives. Teach them and train them. It's crucial and something you're uniquely qualified to do. Talk to God about them. Do spiritual battle on their behalf. The world is tugging at our children's hearts, pulling them down and away from God. So take time to be with them. Share the Bible— children love to hear the stories of heroes and people who love God. Tell them about Jesus…about how He loves them and came to help them. Teach your sons and daughters to pray. And try your best—with the Lord's help—to model godliness. The most valuable gift you can give your family is a good example.

Father, help me show my husband and my children my enthusiasm for You. Through the joy I have in You, I want to draw them in…to spark in their hearts a passion for loving and worshiping You. Amen.

Wisdom and Understanding

"I wish I felt better about going back to work. We need the money, that's for sure, but I just don't feel good about it." Wisdom and understanding can be found in the Bible book of Proverbs. Wisdom weighs all the options and then makes the right decision: If I go back to work full-time, what'll happen to my marriage, my children, my family's home life, my involvement at church? If I spend our money on this, what happens next month? If I fail to discipline my children now, what's next? If I waste my time today, what happens to my goals? If I watch or read this, how will it impact my spiritual life? Making decisions based on future ramifications is a discipline that takes effort. But the reward is a more satisfying life filled with wisdom and love.

Lord, give me a heart that can discern the right paths to take, the right decisions to make, the right options to choose. Thank You for giving me Your Word as a perfect guide. Amen.

A Radical Commitment

Purity is an old-fashioned concept these days. But it's still very much in style with God! I'm asking you today to make a radical commitment. Do away with any behaviors that will cause problems for you, your loved ones, and other people in your life. Be radical about your purity. Saying yes to God means saying no to anything that offends His holiness. Impurity is a real threat and a sobering issue. If you want to love and serve God wholeheartedly, you must become what Proverbs 31:27 calls a woman who "watches over the ways of her household." A woman ever vigilant against all that doesn't meet God's holy standards. And as godly moms, we're to train our daughters and our sons in the way they should go too…in God's way!

Lord, radio, TV, books, movies, even some people I know encourage or accept as normal and natural behavior what You've declared unholy. Keep me strong and humble as I follow Your precepts and model them to those You put in my life. Amen.

Just Forget It

❖

"It's like having flashbacks. I remember what I did...what I was...and I just feel guilty and sad!" Have you felt this way? It may surprise you, but God wants you to move on from the suffering of the past. He doesn't want the circumstances of life to weigh you down with guilt or bitterness, to rob you of joy or cause you to question Him and His goodness. Whatever suffering you've experienced and whenever it happened—whether 20 years ago or two minutes ago—God's remedy is the same. Forget what lies behind and press forward (Philippians 3:13-14). Let the past go. You've given it to God. You've repented. You've been forgiven and comforted. Now move on. Don't let the pain or the questions come back.

Father, thank You for taking care of my sin and all the heartbreak from my past. Fill me with Your joy and peace as I move forward in You. Amen.

Never Say Die

❋

Are you contemplating retiring? Have you already retired? Are you a retirement wannabe? Remember that you may not be working in a profession or career, but there's no retiring from the Christian life. That's not in God's plan. The Bible is full of people who served God and His people fully even in their retirement years. Abraham lived in tents, moving from place to place. He could have quit, but he desired a better country—one promised by God. Moses served the Lord even when he could no longer hold his hands up in prayer. Miriam, Moses' older sister, continued to lead the women of Israel when she was more than 80 years old. Paul spent his final days in prison writing letters that would guide the church for centuries to come. While God may not have called you and me to achieve anything near the magnitude of these men, Miriam, and other biblical people, He does view our sphere of service as equally important. Press on in service of almighty God!

Lord, where do You want me to serve? Energize me. I'm ready! Amen.

When Life Is Upside Down

❀

Is this a time when nothing is going the way you planned? Keep on loving the Lord and fulfilling His purposes no matter how undesirable or unexpected your circumstances are. God's prophet Jeremiah told the bewildered people of Israel in their exile, "Build houses and dwell in them; plant gardens and eat their fruit" (Jeremiah 29:5). Was he making light of their situation? Not at all. He was essentially saying, "Hey, bloom where you're planted!" Serve God regardless of your circumstance. In that same Jeremiah passage God promised that He had plans for the people of Israel—plans to prosper them and to give them hope and a future (29:11 NIV). Claim God's promise to the people of Israel...and to you!

Father, I'm excited about seeing what You have planned for my future. Even though my life isn't all rosy, I know You're in charge. I'm ready to bloom for You! Amen.

Know God

❧

"If I could only be sure God knows what's going on—maybe then I would feel more at ease." Let me assure you that God does know what's going on! When you know your heavenly Father and trust His Word you can lead a life that glorifies and honors Him. Get to know God more intimately by spending time in His Word and by talking to Him. And as you grow to love God more completely—with your mind as well as your heart—you can say with the apostle Paul, "Oh, the depth of the riches both of the wisdom and knowledge of God! How unsearchable are His judgments and His ways past finding out!" (Romans 11:33). The more you realize how much God loves you, the easier it becomes to know, follow, and accept His will for your life.

Father, open my heart and my mind to the truths in Your Word. Reassure me that You're in charge and that You love me. Thank You for all You do for me. Amen.

God Knows and Cares

✿

"God...are you there? Do you know my hurts, my dreams, my disappointments? Can you hear me?" If this is your prayer today, rest in the knowledge that God is listening. "Now this is the confidence that we have in Him, that if we ask anything according to His will, He hears us. And if we know that He hears us, whatever we ask, we know that we have the petitions that we have asked of Him" (1 John 5:14-15).

God knows your hurts, your wants, your needs. He understands you. The wonderful news is that you never have to say to God, "But You don't understand." You can be confident that when no one else knows, He does. You're not carrying your burdens alone! By God's grace, accept every event of your life knowing it is in the hands of an infinitely wise God who loves you as no one else does.

Father, it's so wonderful to know You hear me. I always have someone I can go to—someone who totally loves me. That's You! Amen.

Acceptance and Obedience

Do you remember your mother saying, "I know you don't understand, but trust me—it's good for you!" Even though that was frustrating to hear, usually it was true. In this life we won't always understand why things are the way they are. Newspapers and TV are full of reports about tragedies and pain and sorrow beyond our understanding. And when we constantly badger God we get frustrated and exhausted. As God says, "My thoughts are not your thoughts, nor are your ways My ways…" (Isaiah 55:8-9).

Does this mean we can never question God? No. But simply put, we need to trust and obey Him. We can rest in the fact that our heavenly Father possesses perfect wisdom and knowledge however mysterious life seems to us. Accepting—without answers—is one way to love God completely.

Father, I like to know what's happening. I want to see now what good You're going to bring about. But that's usually not Your plan. Help me trust You and be confident You are present and involved down here on earth. Amen.

Embrace the Challenge

Whether running off to a job or waking up to a crying baby, mornings remind us of our many responsibilities. I can almost hear you saying, "I'll never get it all done! And quiet time with God in the morning? You've got to be kidding!" John 15:5 says, "Without Me, you can do nothing." Embrace the challenge to develop the discipline of spending daily time in the Bible. But what time? Try giving the first minutes of each day to reading God's Word. Proverbs 3:9 tells you to honor the Lord with the "firstfruits of all your increase." Making time for anything of value also means commitment to discipline. Rest assured that the rewards are great!

God, I know spending time in the Bible is uplifting, profitable, and comforting. I commit right now to spending at least 15 minutes a day reading Your Word. Help me keep this commitment. Amen.

Lesser Choices

Do you know someone who used to be really involved in church life or Christian endeavors but now she seldom participates? Does this describe you? Somehow, at some time, for some reason, God has taken secondary place. And anyone of us can let this happen when we make "lesser" choices. Less time in God's Word and prayer. Less time serving. Less time with Christian friends. At the core of our hearts we need to be passionate for God and His Word. When we fail to purposefully and willfully develop and maintain this focus, we begin to spend our precious time and days on lesser activities. And that can lead to wandering off the path of God's purpose for our lives.

I encourage you to do whatever it takes to get your passion back! Immerse yourself in God's Word. Discover His will afresh in your life. Praise Him!

Father, renew my spirit. Fill me with Your love. Remind me of all You've done for me. Strengthen my desire and commitment to love, worship, and serve You. Amen.

For Your Good

Your life might look kind of messy at the moment. Maybe you're facing some extraordinary challenges… or maybe you're dealing with the daily grind. Whatever is bothering you, know that your heavenly Father, your good God, is working things out for your good. Look at your life situation and then turn your attention to your powerful and redemptive Lord. Choose to believe what He says…that the end result will be good (Romans 8:28). Regardless of how life looks or feels at the moment, by faith trust God for the ultimate purpose He's working in your life. Guard against letting your feelings distort your hopes. You have a mighty God who loves and cares for you!

Father, I look around and can't figure out how You're going to take what's happening and work it to anyone's good. But my hope and trust are in You, not in my circumstances. Thank You for loving me. Amen.

The Busy Woman

❧

"I've tried! But reading my Bible and praying every day just isn't possible with my schedule." I've said this…and I'm guessing you can relate too. I've found some keys that help me keep the discipline of Bible study and prayer. Maybe they'll help you too.

Refuse to skip a day of study. God's Word is at the heart of every woman who loves God…even busy women. Ask God to open your eyes and heart to His truths (Psalm 119:18). Make yourself accountable to Christian friends or find a diligent prayer partner. Get up early before everyone makes demands on your time. Something is better than nothing, but always aim for more!

I can do this, Lord. I can dedicate some time every day to learning more about You. Keep distractions from me. Show me ways to isolate myself so I can focus completely on You. Amen.

First Things First

❦

A "flashlight under the covers" book. Have you ever heard this expression about books people are highly recommending? There are a lot of books out there…some bad, some good, and some better. Make it a rule to read what honors God's standards and glorifies Him. And if you only have time to read one book, choose the Bible. Even if you have time to read to your heart's content, make God's Word the first book you read every day. Commit to no newspaper, no devotional, and no novel until your Bible is read. Be a woman of "the Book"! No matter how busy you are, there are some things that manage to work their way into your crowded schedule. As you think about "first things first," make God's Word a priority.

Heavenly Father, I love reading Your Word. Give my brain a boost today and help me memorize Your Word. I want to have it with me…and always available. Amen.

God-Given Time

✳

Is it time to evaluate your activities and the way you spend your God-given time? Maybe you spend time at the gym or bicycling. Is that how you keep your sanity? There's nothing wrong with exercising. Maybe you love to shop so you take elderly or needy women to stores to get what they need. Or maybe you're like a friend of mine who scrapbooks all night long. And how about those Internet hours? There's nothing wrong with these activities. In fact, some of them are very good for you and bless others. But how do these passions fit into your priorities? Are you focusing too much on minor activities? I encourage you to be careful with your time. Make this your prayer: "I dedicate every activity in my day to You, Lord."

Lord, if my passions ever interfere with my love for You or the plans You have for me, let me know. As I'm exercising or scrapbooking or whatever, cause my mind to focus on You. Show me how I can use what I love to do to reach others in Your name. Amen.

Physically Sound

I've been on a lifelong quest for health, energy, and stamina. When I turned 30, I realized the days of my youth had passed. Gravity was having its way with my body! So I began praying for a healthy body. And with that devotion to prayer came more discipline, more determination, and more dedication. The more I prayed, the more God's wisdom became a part of my physical life. I developed a fairly healthful eating and exercise regimen that continues to this day, these many years later.

Did you know our spiritual lives radically affect our physical well-being? Are you trying to shed a few pounds? Pray about it. Need to exercise more? Pray to remain strong in spirit when you're so tired. Be a woman after God's own heart in every area of your life.

Lord, 1 Corinthians 6:19 says my body is a temple of the Holy Spirit. Give me the discipline and consistency needed to keep physically fit. Amen.

Taste and See

One of my favorite books of the Bible is 2 Timothy. It's short but passionate! This letter from the apostle Paul is a straightforward, heart-to-heart, hard-line call to Timothy to live a tough-as-nails, disciplined life. Why? So Timothy could glorify God with his life. You and I want that too, don't we? It's the only way we can successfully stand up to the trials of life. Everything God wants to say to you is in your Bible— from God's heart to yours. Scripture is God-breathed and inspired by Him (2 Timothy 3:16). In Psalm 34:8 you're invited to "taste and see that the LORD is good." Now that's an invitation you can't turn down! Relish and honor the counsel of the Lord.

Father, thank You for making sure I have access to Your wisdom and guidance. Open my eyes and heart so I can discern Your wisdom. Amen.

Press On

✤

"I've lost the same pounds 15 times. I know I can do it again. Please pass the fries!" Sound familiar? As people who follow Christ, our lives shouldn't be about false starts, fad diets, and flashes of discipline. Maybe it's because I was an English teacher, but I pay careful attention to verbs—those wonderful action words. Verbs like *strive, reach, press, endure, run* are liberally sprinkled throughout the New Testament. And all of them are in verses pointing to the management of our life in Christ. Christian living is not a sprint or a spurt. Quite the opposite. The Bible encourages us to embrace life management as a marathon. Our dedication and service to God is to be characterized by a long, sustained, steady pace of pressing upward and onward toward becoming more like Christ and reaching out with His saving gospel.

Father, make sure there are refreshment stations along my path so I can be renewed and revived in Your love. I want to stay strong and steady as I serve and honor You. Amen.

Growing Your Marriage

❁

Growing a Christian marriage and nurturing a life-long friendship takes work—sometimes hard work. It takes commitment, determination, time, and sacrifice. Next to your relationship with God, your marriage is your most urgent and most demanding endeavor.

If you're married, go above and beyond the call when it comes to managing your marriage. That's right. I said "managing your marriage." We are to help our husbands. Ephesians 5:22 says we're to follow our husband's leadership, to submit to him. What else are we called to do? To respect our husbands. And to love them. I can't think of any better relationship goals than these! Of your husband, I want you to be able to say wholeheartedly with enthusiasm, "This is my beloved, and this is my friend" (Song of Solomon 6:16).

Father, give me an attitude of graciousness and servanthood in my relationship with my husband. Help me overlook petty annoyances and concentrate on the positives of being married to him. Amen.

Stick Close to Your Man

❉

"When you marry your husband, love him. After you marry him, study him." This insightful adage is a great reminder to us. Are you a student of the man you married? What are his likes and dislikes? His moods? When does he like to talk and when doesn't he? Let's face it—as busy women we have a lot of people and activities in our lives. But God is clear. If we're to follow after Him, we need to stick close to our husbands. Our mates are to be a higher priority than our children, our parents, our extended families, our friends, and most certainly our work. Our husbands are to be second only to God in our allegiance and loyalty. And it never hurts to let your spouse know how highly you value him!

Lord, help me discover ways to learn more about my husband. Give us time together for talk, activities, and quiet reflection. Show both of us how we can shower each other with Your love. Amen.

Nurture Your Marriage

❀

Remember how much fun you had when you and your husband were dating? And when you were first married? I'm sure you did many spontaneous and slightly crazy things that brought out your love and laughter. For too many women, a lot of less important activities have replaced those special times. What would happen if you put much of that time, effort, and energy back into loving your husband?

The world wants to cloud your view of how important marriage is…and what it means to be married. Keep God's perspective in front of you at all times. Don't let anyone sell you on the idea that anything—apart from the Lord—is more important than actively nurturing your relationship with your husband. God wants your life and marriage to be filled with passion and purpose.

Heavenly Father, guard my marriage. Protect and grow the love I have for my husband…and the love he has for me. Watch over us and bless us. Amen.

Build Your House

❧

Proverbs 14:1 says, "The wise woman builds her house." And that means wherever it is and no matter its size. Whether your place is a grand showcase home, an apartment, or a tent—keep it neat and tidy. Spend your energy building and bettering your home. Make it a place where God is honored and glorified. Create a safe haven for your family. When a home is built with wisdom, the rooms are filled with precious and pleasant riches (Proverbs 24:4). And don't forget attitude! Own the tasks before you. Tackle them with enthusiasm. Welcome the labor it takes to make a lovely home. It's our assignment. Take it on willingly, with passion and purpose.

Father, my home is a place of rest and safety for me and my family. Bless it with Your love. Remind me from time to time that the love we have and the security we feel at home is really rooted in You. Amen.

Just Enough

Whenever I speak on contentment, I share a special prayer. The ingredients call for "enough": Health enough to make work a pleasure. Wealth enough to support my needs. Strength enough to battle with difficulties. Grace enough to confess my sins and overcome them. Patience enough to keep at it until some good is accomplished. Charity enough to see some good in my neighbor. Love enough to be useful and helpful to others. Faith enough to make real the things of God. And hope enough to remove all anxious fears concerning the future.

Contentment is not based on present circumstances. Contentment is based on the person of God. He's all you need!

Jesus, You provide for my needs. Keep my mind on my priorities and guard my heart against wanting more than I need. Give me a generous spirit so I can share what You've given me with others. Amen.

Go on a Fast

❦

I have a suggestion for you: Go on a fast. No, I'm not talking about food. I mean stop all unnecessary spending. And this idea isn't just for those with financial problems. Determine to go a month without frivolous purchases. A financial fast will do wonders for you. I know one woman who saved enough for a vacation just by cutting back on her stops for special coffee each morning. Besides this obvious benefit, being financially prudent will be like taking a deep breath of fresh air. It's cleansing! You'll acquire a renewed appreciation of all God is faithfully blessing you with. And you'll discover new strength for facing and dealing with other parts of your life. You'll never be wholly committed to God until your money is dedicated to Him.

Finances can be touchy, Lord. There are so many gadgets and clothes and things to buy. But You are my top priority. And reaching out financially to others in Your name is high on my "to do" list. My resources are Yours. Show me how You want me to use them. Amen.

Don't Give Up on Family

Being a loving mother, a doting grandmother, a gracious aunt, a caring cousin sometimes means we're inconvenienced. A son needs picked up at band practice, a granddaughter needs a ride to the soccer field, a nephew or niece wants to go camping. How blessed you are to be involved in family life! It's such a privilege to love and pray for the young people in your life. After all, they're your kin—and you have a responsibility to care deeply for and about them. God meant for the family to be important, a passion, a pursuit.

Take inventory. Is there any family member you're skimping on in the Love Department? Is there someone you're not praying for? Yes, I know some people are very difficult. Look to the Lord for help. Don't give up on being a friend to family.

Heavenly Father, thank You for my family. Even when they frustrate me it's a blessing to have them in my life. It's wonderful to know I'm loved...and, through You, I can love them back. Amen.

Give with Purpose

✤

The Bible says "to give as you purpose in your heart," not grudgingly or out of necessity (2 Corinthians 9:7). Another way to put this is, "Let everyone give as her heart tells her." It's kind of hard to give "with purpose" when you don't plan how much to give or who to give to. Intentional giving pleases God. God weighs the heart, not the offering. He's more concerned about the giver than about the gift. The woman who gives much out of the little she has honors God and sacrifices more than the woman who casually gives because she has so much she won't miss it. We're instructed to think about our giving, pray about the amount, search our hearts, and make a decision. We're to give regularly, prayerfully, and purposefully.

Jesus, my finances are in Your hands. I want to be a good steward of the blessings You shower on me. Show me people I can help, organizations I can contribute to, and ways I can assist others. Amen.

Ministry Partners

❀

"It sounds interesting. But I'm just not a committee person. It takes too much time, and I'm busy enough already." Sound familiar? I can't tell you the number of times women have said the same thing to me. And then there are the times I've said it to others. But trust me—serving is a blessing! When you and someone else minister together, a deep level friendship is often born. You might be serving on a committee, setting up an event, or whatever, and a firm bond is established. What a blessing! Friendships based on service to God, on prayer together, on the study of God's Word are oh so rewarding. Once you've tasted a friendship formed with a ministry partner you'll want that element in all your friendships. As well you should. Soul partners and ministry partners. It's one of the best aspects of serving God!

Jesus, open my eyes to people around me. Guide me to someone I can relate to and be honest with. Use our friendship to meet our needs...and help others. Friends are a delightful side-effect of ministry. Amen.

Think on These Things

God has requirements for your thought life. Check out Philippians 4:8—"Whatever things are true... noble...just...pure...meditate on these things." So when you hear some "news" or come across information, ask yourself these important questions: Is it true? Is it just a rumor or suspicion? Would sharing it be noble? Would it reflect my Christian principles? Is it shoddy, cheap, beneath my dignity as a woman of God? Consider again the words *true, noble, just, pure, lovely, good, virtuous,* and *praiseworthy.* Say them out loud. Let their goodness roll through your mind and soul. Whatever you come across, choose to think on the things that speak the best of you, of God, and of others.

Father, keep my heart and mind pure. I want my thoughts to please You, and I want the words they provoke to encourage, build up, and show Your love to others. Amen.

Pass It On

❧

Generally speaking, it's common knowledge that we retain approximately 10 percent of what we hear. Forty percent of what we write down and 60 percent of what we memorize usually stays with us. Surprisingly, we retain close to 100 percent of what we teach to others. You may not be a teacher who stands up in front of a class, but share what you know. Titus 2:3 says you and I are called to be "teachers of good things." Let other women in on what it means to be a believer in Christ. Reveal what you know about living your life according to God's plan. Don't waste all that mental energy to learn something only to file it away. There are so many people who need what you've learned. Pass it on. That's discipleship!

Father, thank You for the insights You've given me. Open up opportunities for me to share what I know and give me the courage to follow though. Amen.

Chocolate Chip Cookie Love

❈

There's nothing that thrills my mother's heart more than two or three little ones sharing chocolate chip cookies at my house. As humans we have so little control over most of the events of our lives, but we do have a measure of say in establishing the atmosphere of our homes. And that includes filling the house with the wonderful aroma of chocolate chip cookies baking in the oven…just waiting for little hands to grab. What is under your roof reflects your love for your family and friends. Cherish and manage it as a place to love your family. If you're feeling overwhelmed by housework and upkeep—take heart. Creating a home is done one step at a time, one day at a time—one cookie at a time! Begin today.

Father, I so enjoy creating happy moments for my children and their friends. Show me how I can make my house even more comfortable so people will feel welcome and safe the moment they step in the door. Amen.

Use Your Mind Wisely

How do you use your mind? Think about it. What do you spend your energy on? I'm not saying you shouldn't relax with a good TV program or a book once in a while. But how disciplined are you? Matthew 12:34 says, "Out of the abundance of the heart the mouth speaks." What you put into your heart will most surely come out. Believe me—I'm also pointing at myself right now. We need to be selective. We need to guard our hearts and minds. Life's too short and too precious to be wasted on anything that doesn't help us live out God's plan and purpose for our lives.

Father, I appreciate the downtime You give me. My desire is to fill my mind with thoughts of You and the beauty of Your creation. Amen.

A Heart of Prayer

❉

I remember my tenth spiritual anniversary so clearly. Resting before God, I was rejoicing in a decade of being His child. Overwhelmed with gratitude, I lifted my heart and prayed, "Lord, what do You see missing from my Christian life?" God responded immediately by focusing my mind on my prayer life. That spiritual birthday I reached for a book of blank pages that had been a gift and wrote: "I purpose to spend the next ten years developing a meaningful prayer life." I was surprised by the blessings that blossomed in my heart. The hymn by Johnson Oatman Jr. says, "Count your blessings, name them one by one, and it will surprise you what the Lord hath done." Such sweet music for the soul!

Father, today I praise You. Hear my voice and heart as I raise them up to You in worship and thanksgiving. You are so merciful...gracious...giving. I'm in awe of what You've done and how You willingly get involved in my life. Amen.

Sparkly Jewels

❦

"She told me what I needed to hear—but it was still difficult. At least I know now what to work on!"

Most gems are hard stones. They're rough and need to be cut. All the flaws, all that's unlovely about them, have to be removed. But once cut—watch out! They sparkle like fire. Your "sparkle" comes by the same process. God, the Master craftsman, holds your heart in His hands. He knows your desire to be a woman who fully loves Him. He knows your deep desire to be like a priceless jewel. But there's a price to pay for that kind of beauty. Yield to Him the flaws in your life that are covering up your sparkle, your fire. Let God work His beauty makeover process in you. Proverbs 31:10 says your "worth is far above rubies." Wow!

Father, I love the idea that You're making me into a valuable gem. But the process is painful at times. Help me focus on You and remember that the end result is becoming more like Your Son, Jesus. Amen.

Consult God's Word

❁

"I just don't know what to do. What if I make the wrong choice?" We all ask this question at times. How can we know God's will? Make the right decision? Truly our first thought should be, What does God's Word say about this situation, this choice? Always consult God's Word. Acts 17:10-11 says the Christians in Berea searched the Scriptures daily to find out the truth. Also, remember to pray about your situation. And how much do you pray? However much it takes to know God's will! Don't rush. Very few situations call for on-the-spot decision making. Consult God's Word and wait on Him in prayer. Psalm 33:11 says, "The counsel of the LORD stands forever, the plans of His heart to all generations."

Heavenly Father, how wonderfully You've taken care of my needs. You've given me Your Word to study and made Yourself available to me through prayer. You are amazing! Amen.

Waiting!

❊

Waiting! It's so hard for us in today's instant-access society. Did I say it's hard? In fact, it seems impossible at times. But what happens while you and I wait on the Lord? For one, waiting gives us an opportunity to develop our trust in the Lord. We're forced to come to grips with the fact that He—and He alone—knows what He's doing. Waiting helps us grow in patience. We wait—wait—and wait some more…until finally we're content just to be with the Lord. And waiting energizes us for the walk (or the race!) ahead. Are you waiting? Welcome it! No matter how it looks or feels, rejoice in your waiting time because you get to spend it with the Lord!

Father, You know my temperament. You know how I hate to wait for anything or anybody. Grant me patience as I wait for Your wisdom. Also give me a gentle spirit when I have to wait for people. Amen.

Keep on Walking

❧

Have you ever been scared? Have you experienced those dark times when you wonder if life will ever again be the same? I have. Five years of wanting children and not being able to have any. A year of watching my father die. Being a stranger in a strange land. A battery of tests for cancer. Yes, I've been terrified and stretched. But I can now praise God for those dark times. Why? Because I know something of God's promised presence. He was there with me. He enabled me to walk through the valley of the shadow of death, just like the Bible describes (Psalm 23:4). So keep on walking. You can do it! Don't falter. Don't pause. Walk! Know that the Lord is beside you to give you comfort and to guide you.

Father, Your Word says to be anxious for nothing. That's so hard. When I'm troubled, let me feel Your presence. Open my heart to Your counsel and comfort. Amen.

Friendships Take Time

"I've been at that church for nearly a year, and I still don't know one person I'd call a friend." That's so sad. We all need friends…casual friends, close friends, best friends. On any given day, many people cross your path. Don't be afraid to reach out, to include them in your activities. Think of them as friends sent by God. Consider them part of the purpose for your day. Perhaps they need a smile of encouragement. For others, a touch, a hug, or a kind word will draw them in. Maybe you can call someone to offer a cheerful greeting. As you manage your time and your life— all your projects and priorities—build in time for people…for their sakes and for yours. Be a friend to all…and cultivate several close friends as well.

Jesus, thank You for the people You've brought into my life. Help me give graciously when they need support. Let me encourage them with Your love and wisdom. If You know someone who needs a friend, send her my way! Amen.

Cry Out to God

❀

Do you know people who don't like you? Has anyone ever said anything negative about you or cut you off or left you out? Try reading through the psalms for comfort. You'll be amazed by how much of the poetry centers on David's bouts with his enemies. He moans to God, wondering how long they will ruin his reputation (Psalm 4:2).

Enemies seem to be a fact of life, but we're not to hate them or fear them or even fight them. We're to cry out to God. Then we're to pray for our enemies... and pray about them. The good news is your foes will never achieve victory. God is watching over you (Numbers 14:9). And He promises to avenge you if needed (Deuteronomy 32:35). No one can frustrate God's plan or His promised protection and victory for your life.

Dear Jesus, it surprises and hurts me when I find out someone doesn't like me. Please open a path of communication so we can resolve any problems. And if that doesn't happen, thank You for watching over me. Amen.

A Gentle and Quiet Spirit

❀

When I suggest the concept of a gentle and quiet spirit, I'm often met with the words, "You've got to be kidding! I can't be like that!" That would be true... except you have God's two great enablers—grace and peace—to help you. God has graced you with these gifts, giving you the assurance that you can live like this. Psalm 34:8 says, "Oh, taste and see that the LORD is good; blessed is the [woman] who trusts in Him." As you "put on" God's gentle and quiet spirit, as you rely on Him instead of your own efforts and emotions, you'll experience the goodness of the Lord.

Jesus, You want me to have a gentle and quiet spirit in the midst of the chaos that surrounds me? Okay. I'm sitting down with You now. Open my heart and flood me with Your peace. Amen.

Suffering

❦

Suffering is a sad fact of life on earth. I so wish it weren't true. Jesus said, "In the world you will have tribulation" (John 16:33). But isn't it wonderful that He went on to add that we should "be of good cheer" because He has "overcome the world"? You can even experience great joy in your trials by looking forward to experiencing great glory with Jesus. I'm not making light of suffering. It's painful and hard. But by God's grace you can look to the Lord. He knows what it's like to suffer, "for we do not have a High Priest who cannot sympathize with our weaknesses, but was in all points tempted as we are, yet without sin" (Hebrews 4:15-16). So turn to Jesus today. Receive His love. Accept His comfort. Experience His glory.

Lord Jesus, life is such an interesting mix of joy and sorrow, pleasure and pain. When the suffering comes, remind me that You are my strength and deliverer. Amen.

A Heart of Humility

❦

Are you praying about a situation...but God doesn't seem to be doing anything about it? Be assured that God is always at work! He's directing the course of events to bring about His perfect will...in His perfect time. That's the difficult part, isn't it? God's timing! I can't say it too often: Read your Bible regularly! God's Word will help you understand His will for your life. Pray regularly. Prayer helps you bring your will in line with God's will. Worship regularly. Times of quiet before God allow Him to teach you. And serve others regularly. Your family first...and then everyone who crosses your path. These "regular" events in your life will keep you depending upon God and trusting His will for your life. Humbly come before Him, knowing He is the one and only God and that He loves you.

Father, You are an awesome God who watches over everything. Nothing happens that You don't know about. I will patiently wait on You for the answers to my prayers. I trust You. Amen.

Earnestly Seek Him

❈

Are you contemplating a makeover so you'll look better and be listened to and appreciated more? My friend, God will use you just the way you are. Too many women think they're not special, that they're deficient in ways the world thinks are essential. You see it all the time on popular TV shows. The ugly duckling becomes a beautiful swan and life gets all rosy. Better clothes, better makeup, a new nose, a better pedigree…the list of potential "improvements" goes on and on. But if you love God and obey Him because of your love, you will enjoy God's favor. Do you want to do extraordinary things for God? Simply follow Him wholeheartedly. Don't hold back! Anyone who comes to Him and earnestly seeks Him is rewarded (Hebrews 11:6).

Father, when my focus is on me too much…and my care goes beyond just staying healthy, rein me in. I want to look nice because I'm Your representative, but help me keep this in perspective according to Your Word. Amen.

Consider Jesus

Human pride likes to say, "I don't need anything or anyone." But the fact is, you need a Savior. If you do nothing else today, please consider all Jesus offers you. He substitutes your sinful life with a sinless one. He assures you of eternal life. Jesus will release Satan's hold on your life and bring you into the family of God where you belong. Jesus overthrows the power of sin and reconciles you to a holy God. I encourage you to humbly bow your head, knee, and heart to worship the God who gives you rich blessings through His Son, Jesus Christ.

Lord Jesus, help me never take for granted Your unfathomable love for me. Thank You for dying for me to free me from the power of sin, and thank You for living in me every day through Your Holy Spirit. Amen.

Snicker and Doubter

"You have to take all that Bible stuff with a grain of salt!" We hear this all the time, don't we? TV, newscasts, movies, pundits, so many people doubt God's promises for their lives. But believe those promises, my friend! Embrace them completely. If you're what I call a "snicker and doubter," my prayer is that you'll turn to God and become a woman who walks in all His ways and delights in all of His promises.

Do you need to make some life changes? I love the old hymn "Trust and Obey" by John Sammis. The words fit so well for us today: "When we walk with the Lord in the light of His Word, what a glory He sheds on our way! While we do His good will, He abides with us still, and with all who will trust and obey."

Lord Jesus, sometimes I doubt Your Word without even realizing it. I'm sorry for that, and I ask You to help me always remember You keep every one of Your promises. I trust You! Amen.

The Lord Will Provide

Do you know that one of God's names is Yahweh-jireh? It means "the LORD will provide" (Genesis 22:14). That's a powerful promise and one you can count on every day, all the time. When you feel overwhelmed by something you've been asked to do or something's taking place in your life and you just can't see how you can handle it, remember—and believe—"the LORD will provide." You might have to replace your common sense and reason with faith in Him, but stick with the Lord's promise. Faith will bloom. The "seen" is replaced with the "unseen." Name your greatest challenge and then take a step of obedience and faith to see the gracious blessings of God. "The LORD will provide!"

Lord Jesus, I need You to provide for me in so many ways. Thank You in advance for always watching over me and my family and for meeting all our needs. Amen.

Love Is Important to God

❧

You can't read very far in the Bible before realizing that love is very important to God. To love one another—our husbands, our children, our neighbors, even our enemies—is commanded in God's Word (Matthew 5:44; John 13:34). When God sent His Son Jesus Christ as an offering for our sin, the model for love was set forever. It doesn't get much clearer than John 15:12, "This is My commandment, that you love one another as I have loved you." His love gave, served, and died for us. Will you ask God to fill you with that kind of love? The love modeled by our Savior? Be prepared for an amazing transformation!

Lord Jesus, You gave us the perfect example of love. I trust that as You continue to transform me into Your image, You will help me show Your love to the people around me. Amen.

Learning to Adapt

"I feel totally unappreciated. It's easy to say, 'Serve your husband,' but what about his part?" I hear this from wives all the time…and I've heard it from my own heart as well. So what do you do? Although out of step with the world's view, God tells us to treat our husbands as if Jesus were standing before us. Is that a little hard to swallow? Ephesians 5:22 says, "Wives, be subject [or learn to adapt] to your own husbands, as to the Lord." God is calling us to a love and service that's not self-seeking. Our intent is to love as Jesus loved… and to pray for others—including our husbands!—to respond to God's message of love through us.

Lord Jesus, a lot of things were wrong in my life, and You died for me anyway. May I follow Your example and love my husband even though he's not always perfect or receptive. Amen.

In Everything Give Thanks

❧

When life is good it's easy for praise and thanksgiving to flow from our lips. But when life gets tough, that's an entirely different story. Yet the Bible says, "In everything give thanks" (1 Thessalonians 5:18). Everything? I'm afraid so! Think of it this way: When you'd rather stay stuck in your depression but you choose to look beyond your pain to see or trust in the Lord's purpose, that's sacrificial praise.

So often it's out of the darkness of my trials that I find God's joy magnified in my life. Think of a beautiful diamond displayed against a black background. The dark makes the stone shine all the more. What a great picture of what Christ has done for us.

Jesus, whenever I focus on my problems, help me see them as opportunities for You to do amazing things. And thank You for using every situation to make me more like You. Amen.

Godly Behavior

✻

Words such as "consecrated," "holy," and "sacred" sound pretty old-fashioned these days. But not to God. They speak loudly of a heart and mind set on worshiping Him. I encourage you to be a counter-culture woman, to be dedicated to Jesus. This is how you and I are to live our lives as women with a high calling...a calling to godly behavior...to holy behavior. I know how busy your life really is. Mine is too. Sometimes it's difficult to even think of having time to reflect on holiness. Psalm 27:4 says, "One thing I have desired of the Lord, that will I seek: That I may dwell in the house of the Lord all the days of my life." Keep your focus on Jesus!

Lord Jesus, I don't think of myself as a holy person. Help me see myself the way You see me and to cooperate with You as You transform me into a godly woman. Amen.

You Tell on Yourself

"I'd love to get together with her, but sometimes I have serious doubts about those friends of hers!" Have you thought this? I don't know who wrote this little poem, but it says exactly what I want to share today:

You tell on yourself by the friends you seek.

You tell on yourself in the very manner in which you speak.

You tell on yourself by the way you use your leisure time.

You tell on yourself by the use you make of dollar and dime!

The poem goes on to include the things you wear, the things you laugh at, the way you talk, the books you read. This is so true! Is what you're telling through your actions reflecting God and His impact on your life? Is there anything you need to change? Set your mind on becoming the woman God calls you to be.

Heavenly Father, please help me see what my choices are telling others about me. I want my life to be a demonstration of Your love, Your joy, and Your transforming power. Amen.

Someone to Pull You Up

I've discovered there are three kinds of acquaintances in life. The ones who pull you down. Those who pull you along. And those who pull you up. The kind of friend you want is the one who pulls you along spiritually. A gal that's moving toward the same zeal in Christ you are. Even better is a friend who pulls you up! One that's a step (or two!) ahead of you. Someone who inspires you and is willing to mentor you to greater growth. Ask God for that kind of accountability in your life. Then do your part to be that kind of friend to her and to others. Sharing a daily passion for God's Word is an amazing bond!

Jesus, You have blessed me with such wonderful friends. Thank You for teaching me through them. Help me encourage them to seek You and trust You every day. Amen.

Set the Alarm

❦

If you're going to make your early morning appointments with God, you may have to go to bed a bit earlier the nights before. To guarantee you start your day with love and encouragement, you're probably going to need to set the alarm. I know! This early rising takes discipline when you already have a packed schedule. Write down this little motto and keep it with you: "Something is better than nothing." Also include: "Always aim for more." Once you discipline yourself to meet regularly with God for some time, you'll become like David, as reflected in Psalm 63. You'll hunger and thirst for more time with the Lord. Meeting with God is an awesome privilege. Don't waste the opportunity.

Jesus, I want to know You better and better, so help me spend a few quiet moments with You every day. I offer my time to You, and I trust You to use that time to teach me, empower me, and fill me with joy and peace. Amen.

Rules for Daily Life

If you want to be physically fit you have to work at it every day. But what about being spiritually fit? If you have a passion for God—and for developing the disciplines that nurture a relationship with Him—then you need to be in God's Word every day. It's that simple. I carry with me what I call my "rules for daily life":

1. Begin the day with God.
2. Open the Book of God.
3. Go through the day with God.
4. Converse in mind with God.
5. Conclude the day with God.

As the demands in life go up, it's difficult to keep this focus. But you can do it! Why not make these rules yours? Your days on the mountains of life—and in the valleys—will be sweeter by the minute.

Lord, I want every activity, every relationship, every decision in my life to flow from Your will for my life. Help me think on You throughout the day and enjoy Your constant presence with me. Amen.

Friendship Gives

True friends don't keep score. Have you ever said, "We had the Smiths over for dinner. I wonder why they haven't invited us to their house?" Here's one that's even more sensitive: True friends don't go over the top when a birthday is forgotten. What are other attributes of true friends? They don't worry when a phone call isn't returned right away. They don't always have to sit together. They don't get upset if you spend time with someone else. They understand if you're part of other groups.

True friends rejoice with you. They honor you and appreciate you. Friendship gives and asks for no payment.

Are you a true friend?

Lord Jesus, I pray for Your grace to rest on me so I can love and support my friends without expecting to be repaid. Help me love sacrificially and experience the true joy of serving others just as You did. Amen.

265

Prayer Is a Privilege

❈

When you want someone to join you in prayer during an emergency, do you have a friend you can turn to? Do your friends know they can turn to you? I encourage you to become a woman of prayer. From the opening pages of the Bible to the closing chapters, men and women of faith cry out to God. Matthew 7:11 promises that our heavenly Father will give good things to those who ask Him. Prayer is a privilege! Through His Son, God has opened His door so we can communicate directly with Him. He's our Father and our Friend. The ears of the Creator of the world— the One who can do anything—are open to hear your prayers. God is always available to you, and He's always here for you.

Lord, I'm so thankful for the opportunity to bring to You my concerns about the days of my life and those of the people I love. Help me be more and more effective in partnering with You. Amen.

God's Temple

❧

"Hey, back off! It's my body and I can do with it what I please!" The only thing wrong with this statement is that it's totally wrong. As in incorrect. Mistaken. Not even close to being right. What's the truth? God owns your body. And He calls it a "temple." Read it for yourself in 1 Corinthians 6:19. And He has a few rules you should follow. Flee sexual immorality (1 Corinthians 6:18). First John 2:15 says, "Do not love the world or the things in the world." Stay away from every form of evil (Proverbs 4:14). The wonderful thing is that your body, soul, and spirit have been "bought" by Jesus Christ when He suffered on the cross for your sins. Keep your body holy!

Lord Jesus, please help me remember that my body was created by You, and that I am merely a steward of it. I choose this day to care for my body with healthful food, sleep, rest, and exercise. Amen.

Strength and Grace

❖

"I want what I want—and I want it now!" Go ahead and laugh, but haven't you ever thought this? In the Christian life this kind of attitude just won't cut it. Following God means a life of self-denial, self-restraint, and self-control (Galatians 5:24). If you're wondering if there's any good news...there is! God wants you to live in such a way that His plan for your life is realized. And true joy and happiness come when you're living His way. I can tell you from experience that there's wonderful pleasure in living out God's will. Look at Galatians 5:22 and 23: "The fruit of the Spirit is love, joy, peace, longsuffering, kindness, goodness, faithfulness, gentleness, self-control." The fruit of the Spirit empowers you. Look to God for strength and grace.

Jesus, I want to want what You want, but I often allow my selfish wants to determine my daily decisions. Help me exercise a little self-control and turn my focus back on You. Thank You for Your Holy Spirit, who is my Comforter and Helper in all things. Amen.

Just Say No

❁

Say no. Try it: No. The next time you want more of some tempting food, say no. When you want to turn off the alarm and go back to sleep, say no. If you're working along on an important project and a friend calls and says, "Hey, let's get together for lunch." What do you say? No. To live out God's plan for your life requires saying no now and then. In Matthew 16:24, Jesus doesn't say, "Fulfill yourself." He says, "Deny yourself." You're called to discipline yourself—your body, your time, your spirit. Scripture calls this life a race...so get into the race. Run the race. Stay on course and run to win!

Lord, I want to say yes to You and to those things You call me to. Thank You for grace when I don't say no as I should, and for opportunities to redeem those moments when I focused only on what I wanted. Amen.

Stamina and Energy

❁

"Bodily exercise profits little" (1 Timothy 4:8). Now before you get all excited and think you've found the best excuse for taking it easy, look at the verse in context. God's servant Paul is saying that bodily exercise does help and is at least a little benefit while we're here on earth, but godliness is good for all things. I read once that walking 20 minutes a day/four days a week burns off approximately 12 pounds in a year. That's all I needed. I started walking, and now it's been a normal part of my day for years. I love to see the sun, feel the wind, watch the seasons change. Even the rain and heat inspire me. Stamina and energy are boosted by regular exercise. So work toward being fit—physically and spiritually.

Lord, when I exercise I have new energy and increased stamina. I can use those blessings to serve You better. Help me make regular exercise part of my day. And I pray for inspiration to make it enjoyable too. Amen.

270

What's Going On?

❀

Do you feel like you're lugging a 100-pound weight around? You're not feeling up to par and it's hard to accomplish anything? Oh, how I can identify. It wasn't too long ago that my doctor asked, "What's going on?" I kept showing up at his office with a chronic throat condition. When I finally looked at my schedule I figured out the problem. I wasn't getting enough rest. Something had to give—my schedule or me. Sometimes in my desire to be a woman after God's own heart, I forget that Jesus urged His busy and weary disciples to "come aside by yourselves to a deserted place and rest awhile" (Mark 6:31). So don't hesitate to rest or feel guilty when you take a few moments to relax. It's part of God's plan!

Lord, I sometimes feel too busy to rest as I should. But that kind of work doesn't please You. You are the author of rest. Help me come to You with my schedule and lay it at Your feet. There my spirit will be renewed and restored. Amen.

Priming the Prayer Pump

❧

"I'd pray more, but, frankly, I'm not exactly sure how to go about it." I used to say that. If you could see my study, you'd notice immediately there's an entire shelf of books on prayer. I read them because they teach me how to pray.

I especially love the book *The Prayers of Susanna Wesley.* She had such a passion for God and for prayer. If there was ever an ideal of a woman after God's own heart it was Susanna Wesley. And talk about busy! She had 19 children. (Oops—there goes that excuse!) I sometimes prime my prayer pump by praying one of her uplifting prayers. Somehow her heartfelt outpouring warms my heart and loosens my tongue...and Susanna's passion for prayer becomes my own.

Jesus, taking time to talk with You is one of my favorite things to do. But I often allow other duties and commitments to keep me from a regular prayer time. I purpose to make talking with You my top priority. Then there will be time for everything else. Amen.

Simplify Your Life

❧

Is it time to simplify your life? One management expert said a routine "makes unskilled people capable of doing what it took a genius to do before." It's amazing what the simple discipline of keeping a schedule will help you accomplish. Take a careful look at the life of Jesus. He never seemed to be in a hurry. He was never rushed and never breathless. He was unhurried because His schedule was based on God's priorities for His life. John 5:36 says, "The works which the Father has given Me to finish—the very works that I do—bear witness of Me, that the Father has sent Me." Look at your life closely, write down a plan, and follow through.

Lord, I long to honor You with each hour of my day. I choose to give my time to You. This is another area of stewardship, and I want to be a good steward. I pray for wisdom as I plan each hour of every day. Amen.

Pray for Your Husband

❖

Matthew 6:21 says, "Where your treasure is, there your heart will be also." One of the best things you can do to improve your marriage is to be a woman of prayer for your husband. You'll find an amazing thing happens as you spend your precious time praying for your husband and your marriage. Your commitment to your union will be more refreshed and reenergized than any number of date nights could ever accomplish. When the "treasure" of your time and effort is spent in prayer, your heart becomes consumed with the object of your devotion—your husband in this case. Prayer will do wonders for you and your spouse.

Jesus, watch over my husband. Be with him in moments of stress and worry. Comfort him when he is anxious about any area of his life. Help me be sensitive to his needs and be a blessing to him all the years of our life together. Amen.

Being the Right Person

❀

Marriage is so much more than finding the right person. You also need to be the right person. Genesis 2:18 says your role is to be your husband's helper. I realize that's not a popular message in today's culture, but it's what God says. A woman whose example is Jesus follows His lead and serves. Yes, it's nice if your spouse helps you, but don't get caught up in expecting it or, worse, resenting it if it doesn't happen. Being a servant to your husband is not about your being less than him. It's all about being more…more like Jesus. Go ahead and test the water. Trust the Lord. Make that man of yours the most important person in your life.

Lord, I pray my husband will know how much I love him, not only by my words but also by my deeds. I want to be his helper and cheerleader and lover. I want to be his confidante in every area of his life. Amen.

A Strong Faith

❖

Do you work in a non-Christian environment? Have you heard coworkers and friends say Christians are right-wing radicals? If you haven't spoken up, maybe today needs to be the day. But where do you get the strength to do that? Two keys are strong faith and trust in God. Christians who contend for the faith must be reading God's Word regularly. They must be well-grounded in God's truth to protect their own faith and answer reasonable questions nonbelievers might ask.

Don't hesitate to ask God for His guidance in your situation. For inspiration and how-tos, read biographies of courageous believers who stood up for God. Get prayer support. And when you do speak, do it gently. Say your piece and let others talk. Don't get into arguing matches (2 Timothy 2:24-26). God will bless your words and use them...if not at that moment, definitely later.

Father, please give me Your gracious, straightforward manner when I hear people put down Christians. Allow me to speak the truth in love...and leave the convicting and convincing to You. Amen.

Teach Your Children

❦

One of the joys of being a mom is teaching your children. It's the best! And this is a mandate from God! He makes it crystal clear in Deuteronomy 6:6-7, "These words I command you today shall be in your heart. You shall teach them diligently to your children, and shall talk of them when you sit in your house, when you walk by the way, when you lie down, and when you rise up." Who is to teach? Every believing parent. Who are you to teach? Your children. What are you to teach? God's Word. God wants you to diligently teach your children…all day long…every day. Make it fun so you and your kids look forward to being together and learning.

Jesus, my children are such precious gifts. Thank You for them. Help me teach them all they need to learn to grow in You and love You. I want to be their model for following You. Amen.

Life's Most Difficult Assignment

Changing diapers, cleaning spills, staying up all night with a sick child. This isn't exactly what we think of when we think of being godly. But hang in there! Your rewards for taking care of even the most mundane chores are great. Your godly mothering impacts all eternity! Raising your children is life's most difficult assignment, but it's also the most rewarding. I've been a mother for more than 35 years, and now I'm the grandmother of 7 beautiful grandkids. What a privilege and joy these wonderful human beings bring into my life. But I must say that I am happy to have those "diaper and spill" days over! I encourage you to give mothering all the passion and purpose it deserves. No journey could be more of an adventure, and no road is more honorable.

Jesus, thank You for the privilege of being a mother. Help me never take this precious role for granted. Some days I become weary, but You renew my soul so I can continue to give to the little ones in my life. Amen.

Managing a Home

❁

Do you know that managing your home is a spiritual issue? Yes, you read correctly. I love what author Elisabeth Elliot said, "A sloppy life speaks of a sloppy faith." We're careful in our faith…careful to tend to our spiritual growth, careful to obey God's Word, and careful to maintain the spiritual disciplines of prayer, worship, and giving. So why shouldn't we also be careful of how we manage our homes? Titus 2:5 says we are to be homemakers. That's not a put-down. Far from it! Creating a safe and comfortable place for your husband, children, and you is a privilege and a significant accomplishment.

Lord, I recognize my unique place in our home. I am responsible for much of the beauty, joy, and peace my family experiences. Thank You for giving me a family to love and a home to care for. Help me diligently love and care for them to the best of my abilities. Amen.

Just the Basics

❋

Have you ever considered how "style" fits into God's plan? Do you shop every week, hit the sales, scope out the new clothing trends? That's probably not exactly what 1 Timothy 6:8 is talking about when it says we should be content if we have two basics—food and clothing. I'm not advocating dressing in a dowdy or haphazard manner. I'm not even saying you can't dress in the latest fashions. But I do encourage you to check your attitude. Make sure your "want" vs "need" is clear...and live according to God's priorities. I know you know God takes care of all your needs. Please note, however, that it is needs...not wants. Jesus told us to "seek first the kingdom of God and His righteousness, and all these things will be added to you" (Matthew 6:33). Not a bad reminder for today.

Lord, our culture doesn't value contentment. But You do. And You let me experience the real thing when I seek You and Your kingdom. I want to honor You by trusting You in this area. Amen.

God Meets All Your Needs

✦

Dear friend, are you worried? Do you wonder where the money to pay the rent or mortgage is coming from, whether you'll have enough food, how you're going to pay your bills? If that's you today, I know exactly how it feels. It's scary. The next time you're tempted to think God isn't meeting all your needs...or isn't meeting them very well, remember: He is whether it looks and feels like it or not. Engage your faith. Faith is defined in Hebrews 11:1 as "the substance of things hoped for, the evidence of things not seen." As a woman of God, your faith can be lived out in your confident assurance that God is in control. Do you believe God will provide for all your needs? And the answer? Absolutely!

Lord, I choose to be a woman of faith. You have never forsaken me. You've never left me on my own. You are entirely trustworthy, and I praise You for providing everything I truly need. Amen.

Be Content

❦

"If I had a little more money life would be so much better. And if I had a lot more money, well, I could really live then!" In today's world of lotteries, casinos, and get-rich-quick schemes, worship of money can take control. And it's not only money. Possessions come into play too. Every so often I catch myself saying, "If I just had a little more _____."

The real issue is contentment. And contentment is learned. God's Word says we're to "be content whatever the circumstances" (Philippians 4:11). It's required when you have a lot...and when you don't. Does that sound strange? I personally like the advice of John Wesley: "When I have any money, I get rid of it as quickly as possible, lest it find a way into my heart!" When you base your goals on God's values, everything will fall into proper priority.

Lord, I often fall into the trap of wanting more. And that leads to wanting even more. Teach me, one item at a time, to want less of things and more of You. Amen.

Addicted to Shopping

❁

Do you love to shop? Is buying things too high on your priority list? Here's a new thought for you: Pray instead of spending. I'm not kidding. Create a list of the items you think you need. Look at the list often and add to it when necessary. Then pray over each item every day. Pray for the patience to wait for God to meet your real needs. Ask God to help you discern if you should purchase a particular item. By doing this you'll be blessed in three specific ways:

You'll enjoy victory over temptation.

You'll hold back on further debt.

Best of all, God is glorified when you trust Him for your needs.

Take Proverbs 22:7 to heart: "The borrower is servant to the lender." This makes sense to me.

Lord, praying about things instead of buying them seems like a great idea. I can see how it could change my life. I promise to start today. Help me be faithful in this. Amen.

Your Best Friend

❀

Wouldn't life be so much simpler if there weren't so many people? We all have to manage our lives so that God's priorities are at the top of the list. If you're married, your spouse is to be your greatest concern (after God, of course). He's to be the largest invest-ment of your time and energy. Titus 2:4 says to love your husband as your best friend, a cherished brother in Christ, an intimate mate. If that's not what you're experiencing, ask God to work first in your heart. Ask Him to help you want to be your husband's compan-ion and friend. Then rearrange your life so there's more time for him. Rekindle your friendship. You'll be glad you did.

Lord, I don't always think of my husband as my best friend. I remember days when we were closer than we are now. I long for those and see that I'll need to change my priorities for that to happen again. I trust You to provide the encouragement I'll need along the way. Amen.

Your Driving Force

❧

Next to God, the heartbeat of your life as a wife and mother centers on your husband, your children, and your grandchildren. What will be the long-term results of your life? When I die I don't want to leave a legacy of club memberships, girlfriend outings, or even successful business ventures. I want to leave behind people I've influenced for the Lord. I want them to have a deep, lasting love for God, strong relationships with family and friends, great character, and the knowledge they are loved.

What do you want to leave? First Corinthians 13:8 says, "Love never fails." Love suffers long and is kind, it bears all things, hopes all things, endures all things (verses 4-7). Make this kind of love your driving force. Amazing things will happen!

Lord, it all comes back to priorities. Some of mine are good. I think You're pleased with them. But a lot of them could be better. Help me choose the best over the good and see the amazing things You want to do through me. Amen.

Loving Your In-Laws

✤

"Honor your father and mother" (Exodus 20:12). Does that include your in-laws? What if your mother-in-law is pushy, judgmental, and difficult? And what if your father-in-law puts you down all the time? Well, the full version of Exodus 20:12 says, "Honor your father and mother, that your days may be long upon the land which the LORD your God is giving you." Pretty serious stuff, wouldn't you say?

As a woman of God, you must nurture your relationship with your parents. And if you're married, the same attention needs to be given to your husband's parents. Building solid, loving relationships with them isn't optional. I encourage you to have a positive attitude…even when it's hard. Trust God for the grace and love and resources you need to get along with everyone—including your parents and in-laws.

Lord, I believe You have a blessing for me if I honor my parents and my husband's parents. Help me keep my temper under control and not let little hurts grow into bitterness. I want to love them as You do. Amen.

Best of Friends

❦

The most endearing—and enduring—quality between two friends is loyalty. Everyone's been burned by a so-called friend or two. Unfortunately sometimes those we trust betray us unintentionally or even intentionally. It happens. But the most important thing in your friendships is that you be loyal. You aren't responsible for another person's behavior, but you are responsible for yours. Proverbs 27:10 says, "Do not forsake your own friend." Proverbs 17:9 says the person "who repeats a matter separates friends." In other words, don't gossip! A true soul friend stands by a friend no matter what's going on. I love this definition: "A friend is the one who comes in when the whole world has gone out."

Lord, thank You for my friends…and especially for those closest to me. Help me keep my thoughts about them good and true and kind. Teach me to watch over my heart and control my tongue so I don't become a gossiper. Amen.

Speak the Truth

✿

One of the richest blessings of a solid friendship is honesty. "Faithful are the wounds of a friend," says Proverbs 27:6. And verse 9 adds, "The sweetness of a...friend gives delight by hearty counsel." A lot of people will be critical of you, but very few will take the time and risk the effort of being honest. The hallmark of a great friendship is genuine truthfulness. I hope you have a friend or two who fit into this category!

You also have responsibility. Giving honest input is often easier than receiving it. Sometimes constructive feedback is hard on the ego! But if you don't listen, your growth will be limited and your friendship will remain shallow. Friendship is a two-way street. So speak the truth in love...and receive the truth in love. Let your friend know how much you love and appreciate her.

Lord, open my heart to the truth my friends speak to me. I'm not always eager to hear it, but I know I will grow if I receive it in the spirit in which it is given. Amen.

A Kind Word

❊

We all have "chance" meetings…but you and I both know there's really no such thing. God arranges these encounters. When they occur we may only have a few seconds to determine what to do or say. Be prepared! Have ready words of encouragement and appreciation. When you run into someone, ask yourself, "What can I give this person? A word of encouragement? A listening ear? A comforting touch? A big smile and an enthusiastic hello?"

People are all around us—family, friends, and strangers. Who knows what's going on in their lives. Who knows the sadness, the hardship, the heartaches, the trials. Do you ever consider your words and actions in these brief encounters as ministry? God may use you to give people the only kind words they'll receive today…or the only gentle hugs.

Lord, You've given me so much. Help me embrace every person I meet today, whether it is with an actual hug or simply with kind eyes or a gentle word. Let me be generous with Your love. Amen.

The Little Details

❦

Friendships are wonderful things, aren't they? And it's often the little details that make a huge difference. I so enjoy it when someone lets me know she's praying for me. One friend sent me "a prayer angel," a little kneeling angel for my desk. Each day when I look at it I'm reminded that she is praying for me. Now that's a loving friend! One note I received included a quote from Hebrews 6:10 NLT: "God is not unfair. He will not forget how hard you have worked for him and how you have shown your love to him by caring for other Christians"…like me, she added.

Be that special friend in someone's life. Who can you encourage today?

Jesus, what a privilege to encourage others. Help me think of someone today who would be especially blessed by hearing from me. Give me words to say to meet her exactly at her point of need. Amen.

Ten Commandments for Friendliness

❧

How friendly are you? How friendly is your church? How about groups you belong to? I've toyed with creating "Ten Commandments for Friendliness." What do you think about these? 1. Speak to people cheerfully. (There's nothing better than that!) 2. Smile and call people by name...and if you don't know their names, ask them! 3. Be friendly and helpful. 4. Be cordial, meaning act with pleasure. 5. Be genuinely interested in people. 6. Be generous with praise and cautious with criticism. 7. Be thoughtful of the opinions of others. 8. Be alert to give service.

What else would you add to this list? The idea is to be an incessant encourager. To be considerate of the feelings of others. I guarantee this attitude will be much appreciated by everyone you meet.

Lord, I can't do everything, but I can learn the names of people I'm with every week. I can be pleasant and assist those in need. Help me to do this... and even more! Amen.

The Ultimate Goal

❄

"My goal is to be financially self-sufficient by the time I'm 40. None of that struggling through life like my mom and dad had to do." You'll never hear me put down financial security. But remember that as a Christian, financial success isn't your ultimate goal. First John 2:15 puts this in perspective, "Do not love the world or the things in the world. If anyone loves the world, the love of the Father is not in him." You don't have to "keep up" with anyone. You only have to live for the Lord—live for His purposes and according to His principles. Too much focus on money can lead to less and less affection for the Lord and His priorities and principles. It boils down to what Matthew 6:21 says, "Where your treasure is, there your heart will be also." Strong words, but oh so true.

Lord, I need to check where my focus has been lately. I've been worrying about things You've promised to take care of. Forgive me and help me turn my eyes back to You. Amen.

Mind Your Mind

❧

Are you constantly yearning for things you don't have, wanting to do things not in your budget, desiring experiences not available to you right now? Being a woman after God's own heart is all about "minding your mind." To live out God's plan for your busy life with passion and purpose, you've got to harness the 10,000-plus thoughts that pass through your mind each day. Your mind is to be disciplined for God's purposes and for His glory. That's a tall challenge! God's Word says to think on things that are true, noble, just, pure, lovely, good, and praiseworthy (Philippians 4:8). Read these word jewels over and over. Say them out loud. Meditate on them. They comprise heavenly language, my friend. And God is calling you… commanding you…to think godly thoughts.

Lord, so often my mind feels busy, even chaotic, with all the things I want to do and possess. Today I surrender those desires to You. Help me be willing to let You renew my mind according to Your wishes. Amen.

Making Wise Decisions

Not a second goes by that you and I aren't making decisions. As you listen to someone speak—and the operative word is *listen*—you need to carefully decide how to answer. And when there's a crisis and you have to make a quick decision, be as careful as you can. I have an idea! When there are unexpected quiet moments in that whirlwind life of yours, put that time to good use. Consider your priorities and values. Evaluate whether they're right on or if they need some adjusting. When you have a good handle on what you believe and why, making decisions becomes easier and there's less potential for making big mistakes.

God, uncover my motives today. Help me dig down to my real beliefs—the ones I act out in daily life. I want to let You conform those beliefs to Your desires. Amen.

In Tough Times...

❦

It's hard to be grateful when everything is going wrong. And we've all experienced that. But gratitude in all situations is an incredible quality within our reach because we love God. Be encouraged during difficult times. God knows your joys and sorrows. And He knows your strengths and your weaknesses, your husband's too, and your children's needs. He's aware of all the challenges you face. He knows your pain if you've just lost your job. If you're single with the desire to be married. If your in-laws are giving you fits. God doesn't overlook anything. Nothing escapes Him. He, in His wisdom, is always working toward His perfect goals for your life. And He acts with flaw-less precision. Now that's something to be thankful for, dear friend!

In this confusion and difficulty, God, it's easy to forget that You're here and You care. I know You have control of all things. Now, Lord, help me make that knowledge real in my life today. Amen.

Be Purposeful

❀

"Plan my day? With my husband and kids' input and crazy schedules? You've got to be kidding!" Like it or not we have to choose what to do and what not to do. I have a friend who always crams in one more project, one more event, one more errand. She's always late and always frazzled. Setting priorities will make your day and your life go so much more smoothly.

So plan your life according to God's priorities. Schedule your day so God is glorified and the people in your life are blessed. There's beauty—and sanity!—in organizing. It takes time and effort, but oh it's worth it. And although you make your plans, God sometimes has something different in mind...so be flexible and go with "Plan B" when necessary.

Father, I confess my pride in neglecting to plan. Some days I think I can do it all! Or I've tried to control everything and it's fallen apart but I don't want to admit it to You. Today, I want my life to reflect Your order and beauty. Amen.

It's Never Too Late!

❈

Have you thought of going back to school? Do you regret not going to college right after high school? Why not do it—or whatever you're dreaming about—now? Michelangelo painted the Sistine Chapel while lying on his back on a scaffold at the age of 90. Benjamin Franklin was over 80 when he wrote his autobiography. And if you visit your local university, you'll see students of all ages—young adults, single men and women, young moms and dads, older moms and dads, even grandmothers and grandfathers. Mental development is a lifelong pursuit. Try something new.

Another great way to grow mentally and spiritually is to memorize Scripture. It takes some practice, but you can do it. The end result is sheer joy. It's revolutionized my life in every way positive imaginable, and it will do the same for you. Go ahead, give it a try. It's never too late!

Father, with You it's never too late. You are always knocking at the door of my heart, offering Yourself and Your new opportunities for my life. Help me take You up on something new today! Amen.

You're Gifted by God

❈

Has someone asked you to do something you've never done before? Maybe you've been asked to lead a Bible study, volunteer at a local nonprofit, or host a retreat? Say yes! You're more gifted than you think. I'm encouraging you and challenging you to take a chance and do something different. Use the gifts God has given you. First Peter 4:10 says, "Each one should use whatever gift he has received to serve others, faithfully administering God's grace in its various forms" (NIV). There was a time when I had to step out and take on the risk of something new to meet the call of God on my life. As He revealed my gifts and how to use them, He gave me the strength and grace for the ministry I have today. What gifts has God given you? Use them for Him!

God, thank You for granting me gifts that allow me to serve You and reach out to others. I offer myself to You today, to help me grow in You so You can use me. Amen.

Your Spiritual Gift

A lot of women ask, "Do I have a spiritual gift?" My answer? First Corinthians 12 says,

> There are diversities of gifts….The manifestation of the Spirit is given to each one for the profit of all: for to one is given the word of wisdom through the Spirit, to another the word of knowledge through the same Spirit, to another faith by the same Spirit…(verses 4,7-9).

Yes, you have a spiritual gift! What do you enjoy doing for others? The activity or process of your gift brings joy. Another attribute of a spiritual gift is your service will bless people and you. Your gift will also create opportunities for repeat service. Giftedness doesn't end, although it may modify as time goes on.

I want to take an honest look at myself, Father. Help me see what I'm already doing with Your Spirit's gift to me. Please give me confidence to identify and move forward in that gift. Amen.

A Faithful Steward

"How was I to know she was going through all that! She never said a word. Kind of makes me mad at her!"

If you're like me, there have been times when you've found out that friends were going through some very difficult times…and didn't tell you. You felt hurt and left out…and maybe a bit frustrated because you didn't have a chance to pray or help in another way. One positive solution is to ask God for open eyes, open ears, and an open heart. First Peter 3:12 says, "The eyes of the LORD are on the righteous, and His ears are open to their prayers." Shouldn't yours be too? And be faithful in ministries you're involved in and look for other ways to serve. Opportunities for helping others are everywhere.

Dear Father, thank You for the way You watch over me and care about me. I want to be alert like You in looking for ways to help and love others. Please help me see the opportunities for service You are preparing for me. Amen.

Life Management

❧

Time seems to be in short supply these days. When you ask someone how she is, the answer is usually, "I'm so busy!" But the real issue isn't lack of time. It's personal management. The body of Christ needs your gifts, your prayers, and some of your time.

What can you do to help others? First, plan your life more carefully and make sure you include time for reaching out to people around you. Then pray for opportunities to support and encourage spiritually younger sisters in Christ. So many times in my ministry I hear this desperate cry from a new and needy generation, "Where are the older women who can teach us?"

Lord, I am so unfocused sometimes. Today I'm fixing my eyes and my mind on You. Help me see how to use my spiritual gift to further Your kingdom and help my younger sisters in Christ. I want to get rid of anything that distracts me from Your plan. Amen.

Be a Cheerleader

Some of the worst words in the Bible, in my opinion, are Paul's words to the leadership at the church in Philippi. He said, "Help these women" (Philippians 4:3)! Neither one of the two women Paul refers to was an example of Christian maturity. They were causing enough trouble that Paul stepped in and asked the church leaders to take charge and get them to settle their differences.

Friends, it takes time, sacrifice, preparation, and courage to be involved in any ministry. So let's be encouragers…let's come alongside the people who serve. In fact, let's be even more radical and volunteer to help them!

Father, You've given me so much! Today help me live in gratitude to You and move out and give to others. May I remind them how great You are, how You provide everything we need, and how much You delight in us. Amen.

Family Is a Ministry

❧

No matter how busy you get, no matter how much you have to "catch up" on your Bible study, no matter how much you need to prepare for a work project, your family is your top priority after God. Your family is your ministry! In fact, it's way more than a ministry. It's a special assignment to you from God. Aside from the ultimate priority to nurture your spiritual life in the Word and in prayer, you have the stewardship—the management—of your marriage, your family, and your home. Family is that important! Proverbs 31:27 says about a woman, "She watches over the ways of her household, and does not eat the bread of idleness." When your priorities are in line with God's priorities, you—and everyone at home— will be much happier.

Lord, some days I feel like I'm getting nothing out of serving my family. But I think of the words to the faithful servant, "Enter into the joy of your lord." Even if my family ministry doesn't seem rewarding today, please give me joy in Your "Well done." Amen.

Transform Your Day

❧

How do you start your day? What sets the focus for the hours ahead? I know how busy you are, but I encourage you to take some of that precious time at the start of your day to read the Bible. This simple beginning will dramatically transform your day and your life. Reading God's Word changes your thinking, your choices, your behavior. I can't say enough about this! The Bible is the tool the Holy Spirit uses to inform, teach, and uplift you. It causes you to think godly thoughts and to grow spiritually. Paul says that Scripture is useful for "doctrine, for reproof, for correction, for instruction in righteousness, that the [woman] of God may be complete, thoroughly equipped for every good work" (2 Timothy 3:16). Nothing renews your mind like God's Word!

My Father, I now surrender my mind to You so that it may be renewed by Your Word and transformed. Let the words of Scripture soak into my heart today to encourage me and help me mature. Amen.

A Life of Ministry

❀

When it comes to serving the Lord, there's no "season" for service. Oh, I admit there are indeed "seasons" in our roles and responsibilities, but the service itself continues. It's ageless and ongoing. In Philippians 3:14, the apostle Paul shares how he continues to "press toward the goal for the prize of the upward call of God in Christ Jesus." As long as you and I have life and breath we're called to serve and minister to others. Frankly, the older we get, the more meaningful and fulfilling our ministry should be. Our years of living give us greater experience, greater knowledge of the Word of God, greater wisdom, greater faith, and sometimes even greater amounts of time. Let's plan, prepare, pray, practice—and by God's grace—produce a life of ministry.

Lord, I thank You for every minute, every hour, every day I've walked with You. You have filled my life with meaning. Now, Father, help me keep walking alongside others to bring them more of Your Word and more of You, the Source of real life. Amen.

Cooking and Cleaning

There's nothing you can do that God can't use. From cleaning up to being a keynote speaker at a retreat, you can contribute to and be part of the work of Christ. What can we do when we set our minds to it? Luke 8:1-3 describes a group of faithful women who used their money and means to support Jesus and His disciples on their preaching tours. Martha and Mary were two sisters who regularly hosted Jesus and His disciples for dinner and rest in their home (Luke 10:38). The mother of John Mark hosted a prayer meeting at her house (Acts 12:12). In Romans 16:1-2 Phoebe is described as a servant in her church and a helper of many. What a thrilling parade of women! And what did they do? Cooking, cleaning, working, praying, hosting, giving, helping. Nothing you and I can't do!

Lord, may I never underestimate the gifts You've given me. Help me see how I can offer practical hands-on help when needed. Thank You for the opportunity to be a modern-day Phoebe—a helper of many. Amen.

The Beauty of Patience

God's Word instructs us to "put on a heart of… patience" (Colossians 3:12 NASB). Yes, even when you're busy. When you're shopping, dealing with the kids, settling family squabbles, in a dispute over a purchase—exercise patience. When you see faults in others, when you're annoyed by people in any way, when you want to be irritated or critical and lash out— be patient instead. I guarantee this new approach will surprise and delight your family and the people around you. In the next few weeks, ask God for the strength to overcome your impatience and anxious attitudes and for the gifts of grace and mercy.

Lord, it seems You often give me opportunities to exercise patience. Sometimes I'm in such a rush I don't even notice these chances until it's too late. Help me be as patient toward others as You are toward me. Amen.

Calm Amid Chaos

When Charles Dickens wrote, "It was the best of times; it was the worst of times," was he describing your life? When the days get a bit frustrating with all there is to do, turn your tired soul heavenward. Let God fill you with peace and calm. God's Word is faithful to come to your rescue as you seek to walk with Him during those trying times. So often our tolerance level wears thin at the wrong time—and that spirit of kindness melts away. The harsh words come out. Your impatient attitude ruins the moment. Proverbs 19:11 tells us that "the discretion of a man makes him slow to anger, and his glory is to overlook a transgression." Godly patience shines the brightest when everything's going crazy all around you.

Lord, right now I lift my soul heavenward. I relax in Your presence. I trust that amid the chaos of my day, You are calm and unworried. Thank You for Your peace…and Your patience. Amen.

Be Kind

❀

Be kind. Sounds simple and easy, doesn't it? But it's not always, and we run into people who are disgruntled pretty often. Just the other evening as I was doing some last-minute shopping for a dinner party I couldn't believe how rude the salesclerk was. And not only to me, but to everyone in line. Galatians 5:22 says the fruit of the Spirit of God includes kindness. Just as our Lord is kind, we are called to be kind too.

How do you see yourself? Are you kind? Do you have a heart of compassion and kindness toward others? As you spiritually prepare yourself each day, put on your attitudes of thoughtfulness and service.

Lord Jesus, kindness is a fruit of Your Holy Spirit. I want to manifest this fruit as I go through my day. Help me particularly reflect kindness to my family— and then to strangers I meet. And finally, of course, may I constantly reflect on Your kindness—for You are so kind to me. Amen.

Watch, Listen, Act

There's no better time than the present to notice other people's needs and do something about them. Yes, even during your busiest times. Proverbs 20:12 says, "The hearing ear and the seeing eye, the LORD has made both of them." Be watching and listening to those around you. That's exactly what God does in our lives. He watches and listens and responds in loving care for our every need. Follow Dorcas' example. She was a woman "full of good works and charitable deeds which she did" (Acts 9:36). This thoughtful lady noticed the widows needed clothes, and so she acted on it and made some for them. Ask God to lead you to people who need encouragement, support, and prayer. Notice those around you and keep a keen eye out for ways you can actively help.

Jesus, surely You set up divine appointments every day so I can be used by You to meet a need. Help me watch and listen for those opportunities to say a kind word or do a charitable deed. May others see Your goodness in my outstretched hands. Amen.

The Things of God

❦

Redeeming your time is so important. What do I mean? Time is redeemed when you make the most of your life by fulfilling God's purposes. As you line up your life and seize every opportunity for useful service, your life takes on an efficient quality. That may be difficult to imagine since you're so busy, but as you focus on doing the business of God, time expands. I don't know who wrote this poem, but it's so true:

> I have only just a minute.
> Only sixty seconds in it…
> Just a tiny little minute.
> But eternity is in it.

As your heart becomes more dedicated to God, you'll reclaim, recover, retrieve, rescue, and regain the minutes, hours, and days of your life for His glory.

Jesus, what a precious gift time is! Please keep me aware of my stewardship of this great award. Help me make good use of every hour, realizing that once spent, it can never be returned to me. Amen.

Guard Your Time

❧

What stole your day from you today? Was it putting off something you knew you should do? Something important for living out God's plan for your life? It's been said, "If you don't plan your day, someone else will plan it for you." Who's the best person to create your schedule? You, of course! Who has prayed through your priorities and desires to do God's will? It's you again, dear friend. Don't let someone plan your day who is clueless about your goals and your God-given desires and priorities. God has given you today to serve Him. Plan your day. Schedule your day. Protect your day.

Lord, surely You have set the hours of my day before me. Help me guard them diligently, making the most of each moment. Give me wisdom as I plan the many details of my busy life. Most of all, keep me mindful of You in the midst of everything I have to do. Amen.

A "Today" Resolution

❀

You don't have to wait until New Year's Day to make a resolution about your schedule. Why not make one today? First, pray over your priorities: "Lord, what is Your will for me at this time of my life?" Now plan through your priorities and prepare a schedule: "Lord, when should I do the things that live out these priorities today?" Ask the Lord to give you direction for your day: "Lord, I only have a limited time left in my day. What do I need to focus on?" Prepare for tomorrow: "Lord, how can I better live out Your plan for my life?" Let the Lord know you appreciate Him: "Lord, thank You for this day...and the opportunity to talk with You directly." Then go forth with confidence and joy.

Lord, my life is Yours. I want to please You in everything I do. I need Your guidance and strength and stamina. I love You. Amen.

A Present for You

❀

I want to give you two presents right now: the gift of encouragement…and applause for a job well done in caring for your home. As one person put it, "The greatest priority in a home should be love. If a wife loves her husband and her children, she is well on the way to making the marriage and the home a success." Proverbs 9:1 says, "Wisdom has built her house, she has hewn out her seven pillars." It took me a while to discover there's no greater task, responsibility, and privilege in this world than to make a house a home. I know that takes work, which is not always appreciated. I truly honor what it takes to be a woman, a wife, and a mother today. Thank you for all you do to take care of yourself and your family. I pray that God will continue to bless you richly.

Lord, I thank You for the house I call home. Give me insight and wisdom in making my home reflect Your presence. You are welcome here! Amen.

A Special Time

❊

Why not plan a special night for your family? If you're not married, get friends together. Give everyone plenty of notice, especially if teens are involved. When the time comes around, prepare a festive meal, go out to dinner, or order pizza!

Later, gather around and have everyone share what they've done in the past three months that was fun and meaningful. Encourage each person to share a goal or dream…and be supportive. Dreams aren't always based on current reality. Talk about the childhood antics of the kids, how you and your husband grew up, what your parents did, where your grandparents lived. Share your faith experiences…and let others share theirs. End your time together by drawing people's names out of a hat and committing to doing two nice things for that person during the week.

Lord, You've given me a wonderful family and awesome friends. I delight in being with these people You've given me to cherish…and I especially delight in You. Amen.

315

No More Gossip

❦

"No more gossip." What an admirable goal! One of the most common questions I get from women centers around gossiping: "How can I avoid sharing it and listening to it?" Philippians 4:8 says, "Whatever things are true...noble...just...pure...meditate on these things." In other words think godly thoughts about others. And if any of your thoughts about others don't measure up to God's guidelines, they're out! Confess them, deal with them, and be done with them. A powerful truth is that if we love the Lord, love His Word, love His people, and love one another, we won't want to gossip. It's that simple...and that important.

Lord, You hate gossip! You abhor words that diminish another person. Help me look at others through Your eyes and think only the best about them, especially when awkward situations arise. I don't want others to gossip about me, so I choose not to gossip about them. Amen.

Love Is a Decision

Loving your husband is a daily choice. Love may start out as a good feeling, but to love someone long-term is an act of the will. It means loving someone even when he may not be lovable at that particular moment. Hopefully your husband is your best friend. Enjoy being with him. Spoil him. Think about him. Pray for him. Encourage him.

But what if you don't feel this way? The question remains, "Will you love your husband?" Do everything you can—starting right now—to restore your love. Pray for him. Do little acts of kindness for him. Express your love in every way you can. Thoughtful deeds and kind thoughts will reenergize your love and revitalize your marriage. Love is blossoming in you, my friend.

Lord, loving another person can sometimes be trying. But by Your grace I can love my spouse completely. I choose to honor and serve this man I call husband. Help me be the wife he needs. Work in his life so he will be all You envisioned. Amen.

Your Attitudes and Actions

Family is the best place to teach young men and women about God's kind of love. Today let's focus on your daughters. Titus 2, verses 3 through 5, says we're to teach our daughters, our granddaughters, and our younger sisters in Christ the good things in the Christian life, including how to love a husband. What are you modeling in your marriage? Don't be afraid to be affectionate in front of your kids. Let them see and hear that you love your husband. Compliment your spouse and let your kids know you trust and respect him. Don't disparage or nag him. Deal with disagreements privately. Show your children that making sacrifices for another person isn't drudgery. Share scriptures that encourage you and help you live out God's calling as a woman, a wife, a mother.

Lord, marriage is a model of Your love for Your church. May my marriage be representative of that same sacrificial love You have for us. May my family reflect Your values and priorities. And may others see in us the beauty of Christian love. Amen.

The Hardest Work

Raising kids can be an uphill battle. I know that from experience! Although we love them dearly, they aren't always the little angels we wish they'd be. When we don't feel very loving does that mean we're being bad mothers? No! We're human…and God knows that. A godly mother loves God with all her heart, soul, mind, and strength. And she passionately and consistently teaches her children to do the same. No one has more potential for godly influence on your children than you and your husband. Pray every day for these little ones and pour God's Word into their lives. Ask God to give you wisdom as you show your kids you love them. Amid the joy of raising children will be some of the hardest life work you'll ever do. And it's one of God's highest callings. Hang in there!

Father, I need Your strength, grace, and mercy as I deal with my kids today. I want to shower them with unconditional love and support. And I want to open their minds and hearts to You. Amen.

The Beginning of Wisdom

Doesn't being a "wise woman" sound like the person is ancient? And we're definitely not there yet! Well, wisdom doesn't necessarily have a thing to do with age. I pray every day for wisdom in my life. I want a life characterized by peace and joy, by order and meaning. Does this sound too good to be true? There's no getting around the fact that a godly life is lived one minute at a time, one thought at a time, one decision at a time. Proverbs 9:10 says, "The fear of the LORD is the beginning of wisdom, and the knowledge of the Holy One is understanding."

My friend if you have a heart for God, read His Word. God is knowledge and God is wisdom. Live according to His high calling.

Father, You are the source of all wisdom. Whenever I am faced with a choice, a decision, a responsibility, may I look to You and Your Word for guidance. Amen.

Thou Shalt Be Organized

Are you continually looking for your car keys? Have you misplaced your glasses, the remote control, important paperwork again? How much of your day is spent searching for lost items? Careful planning eliminates a lot of stress. So plan ahead as much as possible. Set aside special places for your things. Hang your keys on a special hook (but not by the door!). Create a decorative box for the remote. Get a monthly bill-paying system up and running. As I've shared before, I work off a list I carry with me. And no, not everything gets done, but more gets done than if I didn't have a list!

Organization is more than just physical. Give careful thought to your schedule so you have time for spontaneity. Allow time for God to take you in a new direction or show you someone in need.

There are few feelings better than being organized. Take the plunge!

Lord, I'm constantly wasting time looking for things. By being organized I'll have more time for the work You have for me. I'll start on it today! Amen.

How's Your Attitude?

❋

As you rush to and fro running errands, picking up the kids, getting to work, buying groceries…do you keep a positive attitude? Or do frustration and irritation take over? When I'm frazzled I tend to let go. Losing my temper comes very easily to me, along with the desire—and sometimes the action!—to tell someone exactly how I feel and what I think. But I want to practice what I preach. And believe me, it sometimes takes all of God's strength in my life to help me do… nothing! To not react. I continually ask God to fill me with His love and patience, two key elements the Bible calls fruit of the Spirit (Galatians 5:22). We're called on to exhibit the same loving patience Jesus had. And how busy we are doesn't fit into the equation.

Lord, when things don't go the way I planned or something interferes with my plans I get so frustrated. Help me be more flexible. And give me the wisdom and grace to respond in love to the people involved. Amen.

Joy and Rejoicing

※

"Is this it? Is this all there is to life? When does the fun start?" Do you feel this way? My friend, God's Word can cheer you like nothing else. The prophet Jeremiah reported, "Your words, oh God, were found...and Your word was to me the joy and rejoicing of my heart" (Jeremiah 15:16). Rush to the Word of the Lord. God's peace and perspective are available to you now even when grief and gloom are part of your day. The Bible will teach you, correct you, instruct you, guide you, and, yes, cheer you up and give you hope. Make the heart of your life for God a passion for His Word. Spend your time learning about Jesus. This is what you need for your life journey!

Lord, I'm bogged down. My days seem dreary and mundane. I'm going to read Your Word today. Open my mind and heart to Your wisdom, Your love, and Your purpose for my life. Thank You. Amen.

A Unique Boundary

We all need to take time for ourselves, time to revitalize, reenergize, recoup, and refresh. But may I suggest a unique boundary? A dear friend of mine—a brave one, I might add—shared her discipline in the Word. Donna doesn't allow herself to spend more time in any personal activity each day than she spends in the Word of God. She passed this principle on to me, and I've made it part of my life too. A word of warning! If you get serious about establishing this practice, your life, your priorities, your schedule, and your interests are going to change.

Is that the ground I hear rumbling?

Lord, in my heart I want to make You my first priority, but I don't always follow through when it comes to my thoughts and actions. Help me to guard my time with You more jealously. Amen.

Pray, My Friend

✻

"I'd pray more often, but I run out of stuff to say."
I can certainly relate. To grow in the Lord, the reading and studying of God's Word is essential. And so is
prayer. In fact, prayer is one of the privileges we have
as Christians.

The Bible calls us to a life of faithful prayer, which
isn't always easy. One of the best incentives to pray is
that it strengthens us and short-circuits our tendency
to sin. Prayer also gives us the strength and wisdom to
follow through on the teachings in the Bible.

If prayer is difficult for you, set aside a small amount
of time for prayer every day. Gradually increase that
time as you settle into this routine. And you can talk
to God about anything. No question, no problem, no
concern is too big or too small for Him to handle!

*Lord, calm my spirit as I come to You with praise
and share my concerns. Give me the courage to talk
to You and the patience to listen for Your response.
Amen.*

325

Be Careful Little Mind

Are you dreaming of an ice cream sundae? Or maybe yearning for designer jeans? Perhaps you're tempted by forbidden fruit? Ah, dear friend, you have control over what you think—and you must engage this power! What exactly does this mean? Answer: Disciplining those thoughts of yours. There's a nursery song my kids used to sing: "Be careful little mind what you think." That says it all! You've got to be careful and guard your mind against thoughts that might lead you down sin's path. "Sow a thought, reap an action" is sage advice. Our actions, habits, character, and future are definitely affected by our thoughts. Colossians 3:1 and 2 says to "seek those things which are above" and to "set your mind on those things above, not on things on the earth." Aim your thoughts higher and higher. And "be careful little mind what you think."

My thoughts go astray often, Lord. Sometimes I'm not even sure where these questionable thoughts come from! Help me meditate on Your love and the tremendous joy following Your precepts gives me. Amen.

326

Spiritual Nip and Tuck

❀

I've come to the point in my spiritual growth that I believe strongly that if my physical life is important to God, it should also be important to me. But how far should I take this? What are good guidelines? Makeover TV shows and the widespread use of cosmetic surgery exploit the attitude that "this is my body, and I can do with it as I please." But this couldn't be more wrong! God owns our bodies. They're not ours. The body of a believer is to be used for God's glory. The way we talk and our behavior should reflect positively on Him (1 Corinthians 6:20).

Face lifts and such aren't specifically banned, but make sure vanity and pride aren't the roots of your desire. Concentrate on becoming physically fit and active. Find something you can do with your husband, your kids, or your friends. And while you're out there exercising, keep your eyes and ears open for opportunities to share your faith in Jesus!

Jesus, make me over in Your image. I want to become more like You every day. In everything I do I want to honor You. Amen.

329

Heaven on Earth

❀

Would you describe what goes on in your home as "heaven on earth"? That's quite an expression, isn't it? Heaven on earth! Do you know that your home life is meant to be exactly that? The Bible uses home life and marriage as illustrations of God's relationship with His church, with the people who choose to follow Him. And when you live out your God-ordained roles and fulfill your God-given assignments others take notice and see proof of our special relationship with the Lord.

You have the privilege of presenting a picture of what heaven will be like to those around you. When you pursue with passion and purpose God's design for a woman, a homemaker, a wife, a mother, you establish a home that reflects the order and beauty of life in heaven. An amazing opportunity, isn't it?

I'm only human, Lord. How can I have a home and marriage that reflects Your perfect love, Your perfect peace? I want to grow in these areas. I want to point people to You. Amen.

All Things Are New

❧

Before I accepted Christ I did my own thing. I did what I wanted and chased after my goals. And my marriage and family suffered. By God's grace I accepted Christ in my late twenties—and it saved my marriage. Second Corinthians 5:17 says, "If anyone is in Christ, [she] is a new creation; old things have passed away—all things have become new." Suddenly for the first time in my life I had something in my life to empower me. I felt worthwhile and truly alive. I earnestly started seeking God's will for my life. Through His Word I'm discovering more and more about what it means to be a woman after God's own heart. As I share that knowledge with you and we grow in the Lord together, I hope you're encouraged to study the Bible on your own too.

Heavenly Father, thank You for my salvation and my new life in Christ. Every day I want to learn more about You so I can live according to Your plan and share Your great love with others. Amen.

"I Do!"

✻

Is your marriage growing a bit stale? Are you stuck in a marriage rut? This might be a good time to think back and recall why you said "I do" in the first place. Remember those crazy things you did when you were dating? The laughter? The fun? The way to recapture those happier days is by making sure each day involves the same lighthearted joy. Proverbs 5:18 says a husband and wife are to continually rejoice in one another.

Here are a few tips to help in that direction. They're right out of Scripture, so we know they'll work! Sprinkled through the book of Proverbs are these caveats: don't be contentious, don't nag, and don't embarrass your husband by your speech, your appearance, or your behavior. Are you wondering what your husband's responsibilities are? That's between him and God. Right now God wants you to concentrate on you!

Dear Jesus, give me guidance in ways I can keep my marriage healthy…and growing…and loving…and fun. I also want it to be centered on You. Amen.

Humble Yourself

❧

English preacher Charles Haddon Spurgeon said, "Humility is the proper estimate of oneself." Humility begins when we know ourselves. Yes, we're made in the image of God, but Romans 3:23 reminds us, "For all have sinned and fall short of the glory of God." Romans 12:2 tells us, "Do not be conformed to this world, but be transformed by the renewing of your mind, that you may prove what is that good and acceptable and perfect will of God." This renewing is done through faithful praying, when we bow before God, confessing our sins, thanking and praising Him for all He's done for us. And then we can strive to imitate Christ's humbleness. And humility also includes respecting others by serving them and considering them better than ourselves. It's a tall order, but we can do all things through Christ!

Father, I don't like to think of myself as selfish or better than others, but sometimes what I do communicates that. Help me focus on You so I can present You to others without me getting in the way. Amen.

That One Thing

❀

You may have heard the expression, "But one thing I do…" What is that "one thing" in your life? In Philippians 3:13-14 the apostle Paul said his "one thing" was to forget what is behind and reach forward to what's ahead, pressing on toward the goal to win the prize of the upward call of God in Christ Jesus. I encourage you to be like a runner—never looking back at the ground already covered, but, instead, moving forward deliberately. According to Paul's example, we should concentrate our energies on moving forward into the future.

Where are you putting your focus? Have your goal in view—and keep your eyes, your heart, and your life fixed on the end of the race. We conquer by continuing…so press on!

Father, thank You for forgiving me and taking care of my past…and my future! Help me look ahead to see how I can serve You and run the course You've set before me. Amen.

God's Peace and Joy

❧

Do you struggle with depression? With negative thoughts? God promises you joy. No matter what your circumstances, you can have joy in Him. Philippians 4:4 says, "Rejoice in the Lord always. Again I will say, rejoice!" Rejoicing is not an option. And the truth is that the kind of rejoicing the Bible talks about often comes from a life of pain and hardship. But God's peace and joy will prevail. Philippians 4:6-7 says, "Be anxious for nothing, but in everything by prayer and supplication, with thanksgiving, let your requests be made known to God; and the peace of God, which surpasses all understanding, will guard your hearts and minds through Christ Jesus." God's peace stands guard against all those things that attack your mind and heart. Through prayer you'll also experience the joy God gives—His joy—in abundance (John 17:13-14).

Father, You are an awesome God! You not only give me the strength and fortitude I need to make it through my trials, but You also shower me with Your joy and peace along the way. Thank You! Amen.

The Flawless Word of God

How gullible are you? I'm not asking in a derogatory or put-down way. I tend to believe what I hear, read, and watch. If you're like me, you realize there's definitely a need to discern truth. And that ability comes from learning, growing, and understanding the Bible. You may want to get involved in a Bible study or take some classes to further your knowledge. Memorizing Scripture is crucial to being able to separate fact from fiction. The American Banking Association once sponsored a training program to help tellers detect counterfeit bills. Not once during the training were the tellers exposed to actual counterfeits. For two weeks they handled nothing but the real thing. They became so familiar with the "true" that they couldn't be fooled by the false. And that's exactly what I'm encouraging you to do!

Jesus, memorizing takes time and energy, which are in short supply in my life. Please give me an energy boost and open my mind to Your Word. I want to do everything I can to know truth and learn about You! Amen.

Second Fiddle

※

An interviewer asked famed conductor Leonard Bernstein, "What's the most difficult instrument to play?" Good-naturedly he replied, "Second fiddle!" He added, "And if no one plays second, there's no harmony." We need to be more than willing to be God's servants. We need to revel in the opportunities He gives us to serve.

Do you have someone you work with, serve with shoulder to shoulder? A woman you help as she serves the Lord? The apostle Paul said of Timothy in Philippians 2, "But I trust in the Lord Jesus to send Timothy to you shortly.... I have no one like-minded, who will sincerely care for your state" (verses 19-20). I pray that you'll spend time with a mentor in ministry and in prayer and Bible study. I encourage you to mature in your usefulness. Be content to play "second fiddle."

Jesus, You were so humble and willing to serve. I want to follow Your example. Keep me from being caught up in wanting to be in charge of everything. Help me look for places to serve and uplift others. Amen.

God's Dress Code

❀

"Hey if you're working out and 'lookin' good,' why not show it off?" That's a great question! And I've got a copy of God's "dress code" sitting right here in front of me. It's found in 1 Timothy 2:9, and it couldn't be clearer, "I also want women to dress modestly, with decency and propriety, not with braided hair or gold or pearls or expensive clothes, but with good deeds, appropriate for women who profess to worship God" (NIV). "Modesty." "Propriety." These two words are rare these days…both in speech and in media. If you profess godliness, your actions and your appearance should reflect your values. Good works are a great adornment for women who love God.

Jesus, I don't want to be old-fashioned, but I do want to please You. Give me discernment in how to dress so I represent You well. Thank You for Your free gift of salvation. Help me see opportunities to do good so people will be encouraged to seek You. Amen.

The Fickleness of Praise

Faithfulness is a high calling. And you and I will have our reward if we serve well. So hang in there while doing good deeds and serving others. We're in this Christian life for the long haul. Yes, it's nice to be recognized for what we do, but that's not always going to happen. Our focus is on serving as representatives of Christ, sharing His love and concern and provision, not personal recognition.

As women we're in unique positions to reflect the softer, gentler side of faith in the Lord. We can show how kind and generous hearts, tempered by wisdom and strength, come from God. As we serve, we reflect His unconditional love. What an awesome privilege!

When all is said and done, one of our rewards may be praise, but the greater reward is being faithful to follow our Lord and Savior, Jesus Christ.

Lord, my ego likes it when people praise me for something I've done. Remind me always to give You credit. My gifts and the abilities to love and help others come directly from You. Amen.

Love the Sinner

❦

A loving heart attitude is at the core of caring for others. When a friend sins, it's okay to hate her sin—in fact, that's a biblical principle. But we're to continue to love the sinner unconditionally. We are not to rejoice in another person's suffering or downfall, being glad that she "got what was coming to her." Jesus said in Matthew 12:34, "Out of the abundance of the heart the mouth speaks." Here's a little checkup you won't find in your doctor's office, but it could go a long way in keeping you spiritually healthy. John 13:34 says, "Love one another." Ephesians 6:18 says to pray for one another. Philippians 2:3 encourages us to respect one another. First Thessalonians 5:11 says to comfort and "edify one another." How's your heart? Are you living these biblical mandates?

Father, it's so natural to be petty, to be glad when someone who seems high-and-mighty is brought low. But that's not Your way. That's not how You love. I want to love unconditionally and purely like You. Show me how. Amen.

Parents, In-Laws, and You

❁

Today I want to go beyond the "God calls you to love" admonition and have a heart-to-heart with you about your parents and in-laws. Jim and I decided long ago that our parents were high priorities. We purposed to do everything we could for them. While they were younger, this didn't involve much. We visited regularly and kept in touch. As they got older, their challenges were greater, and we had many chances to serve. When Jim's mother's health failed, we willingly spent our time and resources to help her. When she died we had no regrets because we'd been there for her. The same applies to my father. And again as we, along with my siblings, watched out for my mother. Caring for our parents takes time, yes, and it takes money and effort. But it's well worth it...and pleases God!

Father, it's such a privilege to serve You. And I'm glad You've given me my parents and in-laws to love. Help me be patient, kind, and generous with my time and resources. Amen.

339

Pray for Your Children

❧

Praying for your children is the most powerful way you can care for them. Most times your heart will naturally overflow in prayer for them. And even when they're causing trouble or your patience is wearing thin, a quick prayer will calm your nerves and soothe your children. You'll be amazed at the huge difference prayer will make in the lives of your little ones. Ask God to show you how to let them know that after Him and your husband, they're more important than all the other people in your life.

Be ready to show your love. Set aside time each day to pray for your kiddos. And don't forget to pray for them when they're around. That lets them know you and God love them. It also helps them feel more secure and models prayer.

Praying for your kids is some of the best time you'll ever invest. Prayer is a powerful privilege!

Jesus, protect these little lives You've placed in my care. Help me be patient, calm, loving, and supportive. Open their hearts to You. Amen.

A New Woman

I'm sure you've been in grocery stores, libraries, and even parks where the kids were really wild. They don't listen to their parents and generally create havoc. I can relate to the parents of those unruly kids. Raising children didn't come easily for me, and in the early days of my marriage our home was chaotic. Thankfully Jesus came into our lives! When we became a Christian family, our girls were almost two and three years old. God—and His wonderful Word—came to our aid with practical guidelines for raising kids and creating a loving home. My life, my marriage, and my home were transformed as Jim and I, and eventually our girls, grew spiritually. I encourage you to use your Bible's index or get a concordance and search out the keys to a calm, loving home. Also talk with seasoned moms. You and your family will reap the rewards!

Father, I'm totally awed by what You've accomplished in my life. Your guidance and wisdom have made such a difference! I don't even want to imagine what life would be like without You. I praise Your holy name! Amen.

Love Your Home

❋

Are you tired of doing dishes, sweeping and vacuuming floors, dusting, picking up after other people? I can so relate. But it is worth it! Or at least it can be. You and I know that love is the world's most powerful motivator. So love your home—love being there and love managing it, watching over it, keeping it, and, yes, cleaning up the mess. Love will enable you and empower you to tackle it, master it, and excel at it. Turn to the Lord to fire up your passion in your heart to manage your home His way…in a loving, serving, sacrificial capacity. No task will be too difficult and no job will be meaningless with Him as the foundation.

Heavenly Father, sometimes I get tired of the mundane aspects of being a woman, wife, and mom. But I love You, my family, and my home. Help me find meaning in the little things that keep my life on Your path. Amen.

When You're Overwhelmed

❀

So many women I talk to feel overwhelmed. With responsibilities at school, church, home, and on the job there's just too much to do. I've probably just described your life, haven't I? Believe me, doing all that and trying to fit in Bible studies and worship and other activities related to being a Christian is no easy task. But you know what? The Old Testament shows us the way through Abraham. The Bible says he responded immediately to the call of God (Genesis 12:1-4; Hebrews 11:8). He trusted the Lord, and he moved out in obedience. What an encouragement to us! Whether the task at hand seems doable or not, the miracle of God occurs after we act in faith. Decide to do what God is asking of you in faith. That's when you'll truly know His provision!

Heavenly Father, today I'm going to step out in faith and willingly and joyfully do all I feel You are calling me to do. I know You'll give me the strength and time. Thank You. Amen.

I Shall Not Want

❊

When is your church's next retreat? How long until your Bible study group gets together for fellowship? Do you catch an occasional radio broadcast or do quick devotional readings once in a while? Too often we neglect nurturing our spiritual lives by getting by on quick fixes. If your desire is to grow spiritually, you'll need to spend quality time in God's Word and more time in prayer.

I love Psalm 23, which starts, "The LORD is my shepherd; I shall not want." This so reminds me of my need for Him. Are you following the Shepherd? "He makes me to lie down in green pastures; He leads me beside the still waters. He restores my soul; He leads me in the paths of righteousness for His name's sake" (verses 2 and 3). Are you lying down in green pastures as the verse says? Are you feeding to your heart's content on His provision?

Father, You are my Shepherd. I want to follow You all of my days on earth…and into eternity. Restore my soul and refresh my spirit today. Amen.

Where He Leads

❀

What would you do if God suddenly called you to a different ministry? Sometime when you have a few minutes for yourself, take a card and write these words: *anything, anywhere, anytime, at any cost.* Then date the note. Can you in all honesty sign it? God's role is to lead us. Our job is to follow.

How are you doing? Have you looked into God's wonderful face and into His eyes of love and whispered, "Truly, dear Lord, where You lead me, I will follow"? Do these words express the deep longing of your heart? Are you following Him today? If not, will you?

God, You are my reason for living, my salvation, my comfort, my provider, my love. I choose today to follow You every step of the way. When the way gets hard and I falter, encourage me and give me strength. Amen.

Meek to Mighty

❦

"I used to be so confident. But now I feel like such a loser." Do you feel this way? My friend, God never asks for us to have confidence. He only asks that we have confidence in Him! And when God commands, He also supplies. This is true for every area of your life.

In Old Testament times, the Midianites periodically destroyed the crops of the children of Israel. A young man named Gideon secretly "threshed wheat in the winepress, in order to hide it from the Midianites" (Judges 6:11). He doesn't sound very brave, does he? And yet we learn that God enabled and strengthened the meek Gideon into a mighty warrior, a man of valor, a man of mighty faith (Hebrews 11:32-33).

God will transform you too. Yield to Him. Trust Him. Allow Him to do great things in and through and for you.

Father God, when I'm hesitant to show faith in You, give me courage and the right words to say that will lead people to You. Open doors for me to bravely serve You and share Your truths. Amen.

The Strength to Go On

Some hardships in life are devastating. The death of a husband, child, or parent, divorce, disappointment, betrayal...all are very difficult situations. How do you go on when tragedy strikes? How do you handle what life throws at you? The good news is that God will come to the rescue. His tender care goes into action with His promise to heal us. I love these four words in Psalm 23:3 that speak to my heart: "He restores my soul." Our wonderful Lord not only takes care of our physical needs, He also takes care of our spiritual needs. Isn't that uplifting? You can have hope in whatever your situation because He is a mighty and compassionate and loving God who will restore your soul. Hallelujah!

Father God, there's so much pain and suffering in this world...and I feel it too. It's hard to understand why life has to be so hard, but I'm so thankful I know You. You give me the strength to endure and still praise You. Amen.

A Model for the Home

The woman of Proverbs 31 is a great model for home management. She does her husband good. She makes household items for her family and to sell. She shops wisely. She's very industrious. She buys land, plants crops, and invests. She keeps herself fit. This woman helps the needy. She's honorable, wise, and kind. She looks forward to the future. And her children and husband sing her praises. And no wonder!

Look to this amazing woman for inspiration. With God's help, you too can accomplish much. He calls you to tend your home and serve your family, and you do that in so many ways. But are you doing the best you can do? I encourage you to master new skills, express your creativity, and find new ways to help. Even if you work outside your home, you can make your home even better than "home sweet home." What an awesome privilege!

Father, thank You for blessing me with a home and for family and friends that fill it. Help me be industrious and cheerful as I encourage and serve everyone who comes in. Amen.

A Faithful Steward

※

From basic necessities to cars, from supporting causes to vacations, the way we handle money reveals a lot. What has God entrusted to you? Do you have food in your cupboards and decent clothes for the family? Are you able to buy some luxuries, such as jewelry and going out to dinner? Financial responsibility is part of what God calls you to. The issue isn't how much or how little wealth you have, but how faithful a steward you are of what He has given you. First John 2:15 says, "Do not love the world or the things in the world."

I encourage you to do a Bible study on the numerous scriptures that give wise advice on handling money…and put into practice what you learn. As you live for the Lord's purposes and by His principles you'll find contentment.

Father, show me how You want me to spend my money. Open my eyes to the needs of people You want me to help. I want to find the right balance between providing for my family and helping others. Amen.

A Generous Soul

Are you nurturing a giving spirit? Are you generous with all your resources? Giving God and people your time is sometimes the most expensive…and most appreciated…gift you can bestow. Generosity also includes little touches and activities you can do to brighten someone's day, such as sending a quick note, making a cheery phone call, weeding someone's flower bed, and delivering a bouquet of wildflowers.

I remember clearly the day I assessed my spiritual life and decided I needed help in this area. So I prayed…and continue to do so. Every day I ask God to open my eyes and my heart and to bring to my knowledge the needs of others. I consider it fine-tuning my heart to God's Word, God's ways, and God's grace. With His help I can meet the needs of others and reach out with His love. Why not make this one of your goals?

Father, show me the big and little ways I can share my resources, including my time. Help me think of others before myself when I have free time and some spending money. Amen.

The Right Path

❁

"Just relax. Go with the flow." We definitely live in a time that honors looseness. But that's not necessarily what being a woman after God's own heart is all about. We're to be the righteous saints of a righteous God. That doesn't mean we're perfect, mind you, but we are righteous in Christ: "By one Man's obedience many will be made righteous" (Romans 5:19). This means we're to be honorable, trustworthy, and follow God's precepts, even if that means running counter to the "easy" way, the "popular" way, the "don't get uptight" way.

God wants us to walk His paths. And He tells us in His Word how to do so. He also clearly spells out what He considers right and wrong. How blessed we are to have a God who cares for us and guides us!

Jesus, give me the courage to stand up for You and what You say is right. Remind me that You are my Guide so I don't get caught up in something or choose to ignore a situation that doesn't honor You. Amen.

Praise God!

❦

I'm so glad you're God's friend, that you have the promise of His blessings in your life. In Psalm 16:1, David says of God, "You will show me the path of life; in Your presence is fullness of joy; at Your right hand are pleasures forevermore." God will never fail you or change His mind about you. In His loving care you have a shelter in the storm and a haven when life bats you around. In His loving care you can have a generous heart because He provides abundantly. Use Psalm 23:6 as an affirmation of what you know to be true: "Surely goodness and mercy shall follow me all the days of my life; and I will dwell in the house of the Lord forever." Praise His holy name!

Jesus, I praise You! You've given me many astounding gifts and provided for and watched over me in countless ways. You are so wonderful, so powerful, so mighty, and so everlasting. And You love me. Amazing. Amen.

A Heart for Hospitality

"I'm the kind of gal who has a refrigerator filled with bottled water, a few pieces of fruit, and a Diet Pepsi. Entertain? I don't think so!"

Are you like my friend? I'm hoping you'll reconsider! There are so many people around you who need love, friendship, support, and a relaxing time. Begin nurturing relationships by cultivating the art of hospitality (Romans 12:13). Then open your heart and home to others. And don't worry if your home isn't perfect. As long as it's tidy, you're good to go! Pick a time, invite guests, plan a meal or tasty snacks. Involve your family and prepare in advance to lessen stress. Pray about your gathering and then follow through. And most of all, be flexible and have fun! Your guests will be blessed…and so will you.

Jesus, I'm excited about this idea! Guide me in the next week or two as I think about who to invite, when to have the gathering, and what I need to do to prepare. Help me stay focused and not get over-whelmed. Amen.

Managing Money

❀

When it comes to finances, ignorance is not bliss. If you're married, do you and your husband share financial information? Are you both aware of income and expenses, home upkeep, taxes owed, and such? If you're single, do you track what comes in and what goes out? How can you hope to manage your finances if you don't know what you've got? Managing money, like any other discipline, starts with daily knowledge of your financial condition. We can't be casual about this matter of money because it's not ours! The money is God's. And if you're going to be someone who abounds in the grace of giving (2 Corinthians 8:3-7), you need to know your resources. It's a measure of your spiritual maturity. It's a discipline that makes you the woman you want to be.

Father, thank You for blessing me with what I need. Give me wisdom to carefully manage the resources You've given me so I can use it to provide for the people I care about and the causes You put on my heart. Amen.

Trust Him Fully

❧

"How can she be so mean? What did I ever do to her?" If you're facing this situation right now, I'm so sorry. Unfortunately, we're going to have difficult relationships all our lives, especially with those who don't know Christ. That's the nature of the fallen world we live in. But our hope and strength lie in Christ!

I have a question for you: If God is on your side, does it matter who is against you? Please don't mistake this for a lack of caring or understanding. I know it's not easy to be attacked. One thing I do for encouragement is turn to great hymns. In "Like a River Glorious," by Frances R. Havergal, the words are so appropriate: "We may trust Him fully all for us to do. They who trust Him wholly find Him wholly true." Trust Him, dear friend. He will comfort and protect you.

Father, relationships can be so hard and my feelings get easily hurt. Help me respond to negativity with Your grace and mercy. Comfort me with Your love. Amen.

Be Bold!

❀

People should never doubt where our faith lies. We're not secret agents. No way! Along with our friendliness and genuine concern and caring actions, we're to be bold. We're to be outspoken about our faith in Jesus Christ. And we should faithfully pray for opportunities to introduce our friends to the Savior. There's no greater gift than sharing the salvation offered through Jesus. It was the apostle Paul's desire "that God would open to us a door for the word, to speak the mystery of Christ" (Colossians 4:3). Paul wanted to declare Christ openly and to as many people as possible.

I encourage you to study God's Word and meet with other Christians so you can be prepared for questions people may have regarding Jesus. You don't have to know everything, but be comfortable with a few facts about your faith in Him. Then reach out with the true gospel!

Father, I want other people to experience Your love and have Your promise of eternal life through Christ. Show me people I can minister to, help me be prepared, and give me the words to speak. Amen.

Set Life Goals

❧

Is setting goals a challenge for you? Try it! God's servant Paul had goals. He tells us in Philippians that he was energized to "press on" to gain God's prize (Philippians 3:14 NASB). Setting goals will help turn your dreams into realities.

Several years ago Jim and I wrote out lifetime goals we believed would place God and His priorities at the center of our lives. And would you believe it? We're still following those goals! Why don't you jot down some ideas and mull over your gifts, your priorities, your lifestyle. Ask God for His wisdom and direction. Seek input from mentors and those closest to you. Then formulate some goals and set out on your life journey. And remember, your goals will adjust over time. Just keep your eyes and heart on Jesus for continual guidance.

Father, setting goals is intimidating. But I know they'll help me stay focused and be more effective in serving You. Give me Your wisdom and guidance as I set my goals…and help me carry them out. Amen.

Your Spiritual Gifts

❧

One of the best ways to discover your gifts is to ask God. When you're in the Word, for example, the Holy Spirit will show you ideas for service and ministry. People will come to mind, as will ideas for how to minister to them. I know a woman who's actively building a "Barnabas ministry" based on Acts 4:36. It's a ministry designed to encourage people who are suffering and need support by linking them up with others who have walked through their trials. Another friend operates what I call "Judy's Soup Kitchen." A nurse and cancer survivor, Judy knows just what's needed when someone's ill. So off she goes with her warm ways, her warm soup, and a batch of encouraging scriptures. Faithfully read your Bible and start developing your gifts!

Heavenly Father, You've given me gifts so I can serve Your people and encourage them in Jesus. Open my eyes to what You've given me and show me how to use them for Your glory. Amen.

Why Seek Peace?

❧

"What I need is rest. About a hundred years ought to about do it!" Don't we all feel this way at times! If I asked you to fill out a survey with one of the questions being, "What causes you to seek peace?" how would you answer? I responded to this question quickly: busyness. It's #1 on my list. There's always just "one more" of something to do. Responsibility is next. Tension is on the list too. Stress drains my energy. I'm sure you have your own list of feelings and activities and issues that make you crave peace. Here's the good news! Psalm 23:2 says, "[God] leads me beside the still waters." "Still waters!" Can't you just feel it? God knows your need for peace and He provides it. He ensures the restoration and calm you need to continue fulfilling His will for your life.

Father, replace my stress with Your peace and contentment. Renew in me the joy of life and service to You and those around me. Amen.

Be Generous

❀

I vividly recall the day I began praying to be more generous. After assessing my spiritual life, I discovered I could use improvement in this area. So every day I ask God for opportunities to give. I pray for open eyes and an open heart that will recognize the needs of others. And God began to fine-tune my senses. Jim and I have been blessed to minister to many people through teaching, speaking, and writing. We also love to privately and quietly assist when we can.

The amazing results are that people have heard the Good News of Jesus Christ, people have been helped, and some people have accepted Christ as their Savior! On top of those wonderful blessings, the Lord has honored our commitment to Him in countless ways.

I encourage you to be generous with your gifts, your time, and your faith. And watch what God does through you!

Father, You've blessed me so much. As I share with others, keep my ego in check so that You get the recognition and thanks. Amen.

Experience God's Peace

❧

God provides real peace for us…and that includes you—even if you have a screaming baby, a high-stress job, or are knee-deep in troubles. You may not be feeling much like a woman after God's own heart, but John 16:33 records Jesus saying that even though in this world you will have tribulation, you also have God's perfect peace in every circumstance of your life. So even if at this moment you aren't able to fully appreciate the truth of God's peace, it's there and it will make itself apparent. First Corinthians 15:58 says, "Be steadfast, immovable, always abounding in the work of the Lord, [and here's the part for you today] knowing that your labor is not in vain in the Lord."

Bless you today and hang in there!

Father, thank You for caring so much about me that You know I need peace and rest. Restore my energy and my commitment to You and Your plan for my life. Amen.

A Positive Attitude

It may surprise you to know that a positive attitude and the giving of thanks is willful...a choice you make. Giving thanks is a conscious decision, and it's also commanded by God. His Word tells us to give thanks always and for all things, in everything and evermore. First Thessalonians 5:16-18 says, "Rejoice always, pray without ceasing, in everything give thanks; for this is the will of God in Christ Jesus for you." That's pretty clear!

And the decision to do just that—to give thanks... no matter what...in whatever situation—has a powerful effect on your attitude. Not only that, it also has a huge impact on everyone around you. Philippians 4:7 says the peace of God that surpasses all understanding is available to you and me. Now that's something to be thankful for!

Father, even though You've blessed me so much, I still get stuck on what's not going right and the trials I face. Gently remind me that You're always with me. I want to maintain a thankful heart toward You! Amen.

362

Share Your Love!

❋

This is the perfect time to tell your husband, your children, your mom, dad, sisters, brothers, and your best friends how much you love them. What's so special about today? Nothing in particular…any day is a great day to let those closest to you know how much you love them! Also encourage them spiritually. Tell them you care how they feel and what they believe. And ask God to bless your loved ones and draw them closer to Him.

I have an idea! Make a list of those who matter most to you and tell each one how much you appreciate them. Write each person's name on different days on your calendar and on that day give them a call, write a note, send an e-mail card, deliver a small gift… your options are limited only by your imagination. Have fun as you bless the special people God brings into your life!

Father, in my busy days I forget to let people know how much I love them. Thank You for bringing them into my life. Bless them and watch over them. Amen.

Start with God

❀

Do you wonder what to pray about or how to get started? I have a few suggestions that may help you. Start with God first: "Lord, thank You for loving me. I look around in amazement at Your lovely creation. Thank You for Your sacrifice so I can know You." Consider your relationship with Him: "Lord, what can I do today to live out the fact You are my ultimate priority?" Write down God's answers and promptings. Then ask, "Lord, what can I do today to grow spiritually? How can I prepare for future ministry?" Finish with, "Lord, what else would You have me do today?"

These simple prayers put your heart and feet in line with God and His plan.

Father, I love that I can come to You in praise... and get my questions answered. It amazes me that You care about the big and little things that happen in my life. I know You love me. Help me get over any awkwardness I feel about approaching You. Amen.

364

Good News!

❄

Do you know Jesus? Is He your Lord and Savior? Romans 3:23 reveals that we all have sinned. We all fall short of God's glory. And the penalty for sin is death…spiritual death. The Good News is Christ died for you (and me)! Romans 10:9 says, "If you confess with your mouth the Lord Jesus and believe in your heart that God has raised Him from the dead, you will be saved." Please take this opportunity to give your life to Jesus. Open yourself to His love and truth. Ask Him to come into your heart and be with you forever. He's waiting for you!

And if you already know Jesus, praise His holy name!

Jesus, I yearn to experience Your love. In my sin-filled heart I don't even come close to being as You are. Thank You for coming to earth and paying the price for my sins so I can know You personally. I accept Your free gift of salvation. Help me grow in You every day. Amen.

365

God's Grace

❧

Do you know that the sustaining power of God is packaged in His grace? Life can deliver some tough blows, but God's marvelous grace enables us to go from strength to strength through all the trials. Second Corinthians 12:9 promises that God's grace is sufficient—that it is made perfect in our weakness. I know that encourages my heart. Take that trial you're experiencing and bring it to the Lord. Lay it at His feet. Look to Him. Count on His grace and power in every situation. It's there. It's given to you. And it brings the peace you so long for.

Bless you in your journey to become a woman after God's own heart.

Father, my heart overflows with the love and blessings You've given me. Even in the midst of my trials and sorrow I can be joyful in my heart because I know You are in charge. Amen.

366

Prayer Will Change Your Life

Do you have trouble praying? Are you uncertain whether it accomplishes anything? Let me assure you that prayer can change your life in ways you've never imagined. Why do I encourage you to pray? For one thing, I don't want you to miss out on a ton of blessings! Prayer increases your faith in God and eases your burdens. It opens your heart to His love and peace and encouragement on those days full of panic and stress. Prayer also changes lives—yours and the people you pray for. Prayer helps you focus on others and not yourself, which usually improves relationships. Prayer brings contentment as you commune with God. It opens the path to God's wisdom so you can be confident in making decisions. And prayer is a powerful ministry. James 4:8 says, "Draw near to God and He will draw near to you."

Father, I lift my voice and praise to You. Help me know that You're listening. Give me Your strength and wisdom today. Draw close to me. Amen.

Favorite Scriptures

_____

_____

_____

_____

_____

_____

_____

_____

_____

_____

_____

Favorite Scriptures

_____

_____

_____

_____

_____

_____

_____

_____

_____

_____

_____

Favorite Prayers

_____

_____

_____

_____

_____

_____

_____

_____

_____

_____

_____

_____

Favorite Prayers

_____

_____

_____

_____

_____

_____

_____

_____

_____

_____

_____

_____

_____

Favorite Truths About God

_____

_____

_____

_____

_____

_____

_____

_____

_____

_____

_____

Favorite Truths About God

_____

_____

_____

_____

_____

_____

_____

_____

_____

_____

_____

Favorite Insights

Favorite Insights

_____

_____

_____

_____

_____

_____

_____

_____

_____

_____

_____

Favorite Examples

_____

_____

_____

_____

_____

_____

_____

_____

_____

_____

_____

Favorite Examples

_____

_____

_____

_____

_____

_____

_____

_____

_____

_____

_____

_____

Books by Elizabeth George

- Beautiful in God's Eyes
- Finding God's Path Through Your Trials
- Life Management for Busy Women
- Loving God with All Your Mind
- A Mom After God's Own Heart
- Powerful Promises for Every Woman
- The Remarkable Women of the Bible
- Small Changes for a Better Life
- A Wife After God's Own Heart
- A Woman After God's Own Heart®
- A Woman After God's Own Heart® Deluxe Edition
- A Woman After God's Own Heart®—A Daily Devotional
- A Woman After God's Own Heart® Collection
- A Woman's Call to Prayer
- A Woman's High Calling
- A Woman's Walk with God
- A Young Woman After God's Own Heart
- A Young Woman's Call to Prayer
- A Young Woman's Walk with God

Children's Books

- God's Wisdom for Little Girls
- A Little Girl After God's Own Heart

Study Guides

- Beautiful in God's Eyes Growth & Study Guide
- Finding God's Path Through Your Trials Growth & Study Guide
- Life Management for Busy Women Growth & Study Guide
- Loving God with All Your Mind Growth & Study Guide
- A Mom After God's Own Heart Growth & Study Guide
- The Remarkable Women of the Bible Growth & Study Guide
- Small Changes for a Better Life Growth & Study Guide
- A Wife After God's Own Heart Growth & Study Guide
- A Woman After God's Own Heart® Growth & Study Guide
- A Woman's Call to Prayer Growth & Study Guide
- A Woman's High Calling Growth & Study Guide
- A Woman's Walk with God Growth & Study Guide

Books by Jim & Elizabeth George

- God Loves His Precious Children
- God's Wisdom for Little Boys
- A Little Boy After God's Own Heart

Books by Jim George

- The Bare Bones Bible™ Handbook
- A Husband After God's Own Heart
- A Man After God's Own Heart
- The Remarkable Prayers of the Bible
- The Remarkable Prayers of the Bible Growth & Study Guide
- What God Wants to Do for You
- A Young Man After God's Own Heart

About the Author

Elizabeth George is a bestselling author who has more than four million books in print. She is a popular speaker at Christian women's events. Her passion is to teach the Bible in a way that changes women's lives.

For information about Elizabeth's speaking ministry, to sign up for her mailings, or to purchase her books visit her website:

www.ElizabethGeorge.com

Toll-free: 1-800-542-4611

Elizabeth George
PO Box 2879
Belfair, WA 98528